ROLE AND STATUS OF
WORKING WOMEN

ROLE AND STATUS
OF
WORKING WOMEN

Shanta B. Astige

ANMOL PUBLICATIONS PVT. LTD.
NEW DELHI - 110 002 (INDIA)

ANMOL PUBLICATIONS PVT. LTD.
H.O.: 4374/4B, Ansari Road, Darya Ganj,
New Delhi-110 002 (India)
Ph.: 23278000, 23261597
B.O.: No. 1015, Ist Main Road, BSK IIIrd Stage
IIIrd Phase, IIIrd Block,
Bangalore - 560 085 (India)
Visit us at: www.anmolpublications.com

Role & Status of Working Women

First Published, 2006

ISBN 81-261-2897-6

PRINTED IN INDIA

Printed at Mehra Offset Press, Delhi.

Contents

Foreword

With gender issues having come, of late, to the forefront of academic and policy attention, Women's Studies, has emerged as an academic discipline of considerable significance and promise. Gender issues concerning half of the humanity have come to be accorded the place of priority in academic, political and civic circles that in the recent past was unthinkable. Thanks to the ameliorative and imancipatory efforts of philanthrophers, social reformers, social scientists, feminists and activists in the recent past, the concern for and awareness about gender justice, gender equity has reached unprecedented levels among populace in general and intelligentia as well as academic fraternity in particular. Transnationalization, revolution in IT and CT, revolution in science and technology coupled with cultural revolution and growing rationalism have thrown up both opportunities and challenges for women that a generation or two ago were unimaginable, giving rise to socio-cultural milieu and a host of gender related issues, that warrant the immediate empirical and scientific attention of social scientists in general and Sociologists in particular. It is precisely owing to these reasons, there has been an unprecedented rise in empirical, clinical and diagnostic studies on issues concerning women and social realities pertaining to them. One such commendable attempt that stands out and warrants a first hand reading is "Status of Working Women in Modern India" by Dr. Shanta Astige. This book, based upon empirical findings, seeks to provide new sociological insights into the intricate realities pertaining an emerging section of society that holds key to the systematic understanding of and implications of seminal significance for contemporary Indian Society. Several empirical surveys and enumerations have been attempted in the recent past focusing on women work and professions that are mainly of statistical and economic relevance, but this book by Dr. Shanta Astige incorporates much needed and less adopted sociological perspective in approaching the phenomenon of women, work, family and marriage promising a novel and fresh look at these issues.

The book is a refreshing relook at the gender issues that have traditionally been focused by Sociologists and represents a welcome departure from the routine and stereotype empirics.

The book begins with thrashing out of issues pertaining to gender and several unwarranted and unfounded generations that have rendered scholars and policy makers myopic to the intricate social realities surrounding women, work and wedlock. These forays lend much needed justification for a study as present one and further, a thoughtfully chosen and organized review of literature provides a meaningful and indispensable theoretical and empirical backdrop against which, the analysis of the findings of the present study gain greater relevance and meaning.

The book has succeeded in capturing emerging trends of aspirations, achievements, challenges and constraints among womenfolk taking to gainful employment. The complex and intricate interface between education, employment, marriage and family relating to Indian women has been the main focus which has been quite insightfully and skillfully handled in the book owing to which it makes quite an interesting and refreshing reading, providing the reader with an academically enriching and intellectually rewarding experience. It deals diligently with minute aspects of work life of women and these are interwoven to present a meaningful fabric that provides integrated, insightful and empirical insights into the functional and attitudinal aspects as well as ethos and pathos of on the job and off the job lives, and their interfaces, faced by Indian working women. It succeeds in providing a panoramic view of contemporary social realities pertaining to this emerging section of Indian society. Dr. Shanta Astige is at her inimitable best in this work and this work stands out as a testimony to her intellectual maturity and devotion to academics. Owing to all these merits of the book and its author, it may be viewed as an important addition to the existing literature on empirical Sociology in general and Sociology of Gender in particular. I look forward to having many more such significant contributions from Dr. Shanta Astige, while wishing her all the very best in all her academic endeavors and intellectual persuits.

—Dr. S.L. Hiremath

Preface

As I started my professional career, I began to experience the problems of a working woman. A good number of my senior colleagues in college and other friends working in various offices, too narrated the tales of a working woman. I found that many working women were caught between family and career. It was this dilemma of mine as working woman, which motivated and inspired me to undertake the present subject for my doctoral research

As a fresh candidate, I was quite new to theory and methodology. My research guide constantly helped me in going through relevant books, journals, and articles on different theoretical perspectives and research methodology. On several occasions, he even accompanied me while conducting interviews with the respondents. My research guide constantly advised me to check and recheck the interview schedules, tabulated data, warning me from time to time not to make loose, ambiguous and hasty statements. On this occasion, I want to express my sincere gratitude to my research guide **Dr. Ambarao Uplaonkar**, for his constant help in completing the thesis within the appointed time.

I am greatly thankful to **Dr. S.L. Hiremath,** Professor & Former Head, Department of Sociology, Gulbarga University, Gulbarga who had been my research guide for the M.Phil. Programme, for his encouragement to pursue research for the Ph.D. degree as soon as I completed my M.Phil. Indeed, I am ever grateful to him. Similarly, I also wish to extend my heartfelt thanks to **Dr. M.S. Dhadve,** Professor of Sociology,

Gulbarga University, Gulbarga for his kind encouragement to undertake the Ph.D. Programme.

I also wish to thank **Dr. Meti Sheshan,** Professor & H.O.D. of Sociology, Gulbarga University, Gulbarga; **Dr. Nusrath Fatima,** Professor of Sociology, **Dr. Jaganath Shinde,** Professor of Sociology, Gulbarga University, Gulbarga, for their help and cooperation in completing the work.

I can never forget the help rendered by **Sri. G.B. Sajjan,** Retd. Professor of English and Former Principal of Sharnbasaveshwar College of Arts, Gulbarga, who went through the manuscript and made extensive suggestions for improvement of the draft. I am ever grateful to him.

Next, I want to thank my husband **Prof. Mallinath C. Navindgi,** P.D.A. College of Engineering, Gulbarga, who sat with me through several nights and helped me in checking interview schedules and transferring the data on code sheets. I am doubly grateful to him for his contribution towards looking after the children and overseeing the domestic chores. Indeed, my husband acted like a friend, philosopher and guide. I also owe my sincere gratitude to my parents-in-law, **Prof. C.R. Navindgi and Smt. Subhadra Navindgi,** for the unstinted sympathy and kindness, which they extended to me during the study period.

I owe a special debt to my parents who gave a boost and fillip to my ambitions and goals of life. I wish to thank **Mr. Mahesh,** who sat day and night and completed the DTP work in record time. Finally, I want to thank **Anmol Publications Pvt. Ltd.,** New Delhi for accepting my proposal to publish the work.

—Dr. Shanta Astige

List of Tables

1

Introduction

Traditionally, women in India were not supposed to work for gainful employment outside the home. Work involved contact with men and pollution. Fathers, brothers, husbands were afraid that women working outside the home for wages with men might develop illicit sexual relation and thereby loose their chastity.

Working for wages in the past was generally associated with low economic status of a family. Women with higher castes and classes were prohibited from working for wages outside the home. Women in higher castes and classes were even discouraged doing domestic chores like washing cloths and cleaning utensils.

With the advent of industrialisation and urbanisation the nature and character of work has undergone a radical change. For example, work is more specialised and skilled. A large number of jobs and occupations have sprung up in the field of teaching, administration and electronics which could be taken up by both men and women. Besides, work in organized sector has relatively become secured and remunerative. As a result there are more favourable conditions for women's employment in modern society.

Working Women: A New Concept

The concept of working woman is a recent phenomenon.

The advent of industrialisation, urbanisation, modern education and science and technology in the last five decades has created a favourable situation for women, especially in urban areas, enabling them to take to modern education and employment. Obviously, the emerging phenomenon of working women in modern society has deeper and wider implications for the women themselves, for the family and the society at large. As Desai and Anantaram (1985) have observed, middle class women's outside work participation is not merely an economic activity, but it affects norms regarding the proper sphere of women, their status vis-à-vis their husbands, values underlying patriarchal family structure, redefinition of the roles of family members, care of children, mixing with other men and remaining outside the house for long hours.

Differences of Opinion

There are equally sharp differences of opinion about the changes taking place in the position of women in India. Some regard these changes as profound and pervasive, they point to the increasing participation of women in public life and to the changes introduced in their legal status. (Kapur, 1974, Mishra 1993, Lalitha Devi, 1982). Others maintain that the position of women has changed very little and that Indian society continues, by and large, to be a male-dominated society (Beteille, 1975:61).

Other studies have held that the role and status of the working woman vis-à-vis household duties has not changed significantly. Cook (1975: 28) concluded: "whether married women work or not, they receive little assistance with house-work from their husbands. When they work, they must still carry the major responsibility for care of home and children. Prakash Rao and Nandini Rao (1982: 213) report that neither employed nor non-employed mothers get any help from husbands. It is important to note that Rao and Rao further point out that with employment the household responsibilities outside the home such as buying grocery, taking children to school etc. increase. It follows that employment brings in its wake more problems to the working wife. M. Hanumanth Rao in his article (1990) "Employment of the Wife and Husband's participation in House work" concludes that the traditional sex-specific division of labour does not appear to have changed very much in the families of working women. Husbands of working wives do not share household tasks like cooking, sweeping etc.

A number of studies both in India and the world over have analysed the impact of women's education and employment on society. But there are differences in the findings of sociologists about the effects of employment in altering the status and role of women. According to Wood (1975), employment has fostered in women a dynamic and pragmatic approach to life, an individualistic view of self, and a cosmopolitan orientation attitude, which are manifested in the working woman's patterns of family life and in her changing familial roles. Other studies have indicated that since the Indian society is in the process of modernisation, changes in the role and status of working women are likely to be vague, ambiguous and confusing. Shashi Jain (1988:214) says, "The working wife is not yet clear about her roles. The changed context has created role confusion for the working wife; to her established roles as wife and mother, a new role of working outside the home and earning a salary has now been added. The confusion arises because of the absence of fit between the old and the new role". It is argued that changes in the role and status of working women depend on the socio-economic and educational status of the family members. Dowell observes in this connection: "Students of the family have assumed that adding the role of employee to the woman's role of wife and mother often necessitates a redefinition of the roles of family members in terms of duties and responsibilities". The problem of employed women is how to harmonise the two roles of wife and mother, with that of working outside the home.

A number of studies conducted on employed women have shown both favourable and unfavorable effects on their role and status in the family, i.e. vis-à-vis the husband and the in-laws. Anita Sharma (1990); Kapur (1974) Bhusan (1983) and several others, have concluded that employment of women has brought about positive changes. For example, employment provided them personal status, independent social standing, social confidence and changed outlook. But there are other studies, which have highlighted the negative effects, such as marital frustration, role-conflict, divorce etc. In her study, Jyoti Barot (1975) found that husbands considered their working wives to be more responsible for conflicts between wife and mother-in-law. Kapur (1970) notes that the employed woman does not receive any extra rights or privileges by virtue of her engaging in paid work outside the home. Murickan (1977) reported the findings of several studies conducted in three metropolitan centres of Kerala. He concluded that most of the women in Kerala lived under male dominance and were hampered by tradition, cultural and religious taboos. Neera Desai (1957) observed, in India generally, the tradition-ridden husbands and in-laws are prejudiced against the working wife. The consider an employed wife to be loose in morals and generally doubt her chastity as she has to work with male colleagues. In India, generally, a husband is very much influenced by society's traditional attitude. It means the effects of employment of women on the relationships between the wife and her husband and on other members in the family should be studied in the context of the cultural values of Indian society. Very few findings of changes are recorded in respect of the attitudes of working women towards issues like dowry, divorce, joint family etc. (Mamdaani, 1972).

The findings of a good number of studies, due to inappropriate theoretical framework and methodology, suffer from faulty interpretation. It is reported that educated and employed women tend to prefer love marriages; they are even prepared to go in for inter-caste marriages. But such statements are very general, vague and non-categorical, and based on hear say. For example, in what sense are terms like 'love-marriage', 'inter-caste marriage' used? How many 'higher castes' employed women are prepared to marry employed SCs and STs? However, it cannot be denied that there do take place inter-sub-caste marriages within a caste and very few inter-caste marriages, which could be counted on fingers ends. Love marriages and inter-caste marriages are not yet socially accepted. Therefore, it is necessary to undertake a study of the changing role and status of working women with an appropriate theoretical framework, methodology and sample size. According to Karuna Ahmed (1979) in the Indian context, not only is the empirical evidence limited, but also the existing evidence is inconclusive on the issue whether education has promoted egalitarian role relationships.

According to Neera Desai and Maithreyi Krishnaraj (1988), employment by itself does not guarantee independence or improved status of women, which is proved by the middle class experience where they are better off than their poorer sisters, in other ways; health, education, material resources etc. Fundamental changes are needed in the family structure, work-arrangements and value system.

The Working Woman in India

Research Questions

The main question is: Does employment of woman bring about a significant degree of change towards the equality of status of woman in a society like the Indian, which continues to be traditional and stratified in its social setup?

The specific questions are:

1. What happens to the role and status of educated women when they are employed in the context of a traditional society like the Indian?
2. Does employment act as an agent of modernisation in bringing about attitudinal changes in educated working women towards traditional social issues such as women's education and employment, and marriage and family? Or does it not?
3. Why do educated women take to employment?
4. How do educated working women perceive the importance of education and employment vis-à-vis their traditional role and status as wife and mother?
5. How does employment of women affect their relationship with their husbands and parents-in-law?

The theoretical assumption of the study is that since there are no radical changes in the structure of Indian society, in terms of social class, urbanisation, industrialisation and modernisation, women's educational and employed status is not likely to produce far-reaching changes and shifts in the role and status of woman in terms of equality in Indian society. As traditional institutions continue to have their hold, employment of woman will produce minimal and nominal rather than radical changes.

Distinguishing Features of the Study

1. The study is based on sound theory and methodology.
2. The respondents are graduates at the minimum.
3. The study does not only depend solely on formal

responses. It has, besides, deeply probed into the inner feelings and reactions of the working woman.

Hypothesis

The present study intends to test the hypothesis that employment of woman brings about significant changes in terms of equality in her status and role vis–a–vis family and office. Our assumption is that since the Indian society continues to be relatively conservative, rigid, backward and stratified, a change in the economic role of the woman, added to her educational status, is not likely to bring about worthwhile changes.

Objectives of the Study

The chief objective of the study is to analyse the influence of employment on the role and status of the educated woman.

Specific Objectives of the Study

The specific objectives of the study are:

I. To study, if the working women were becoming modern towards social issues viz women's education and employment and marriage and family.

1. *Education*

To study the attitudes of working women towards:

(a) Aims of higher education in relation to women,
(b) Levels of education for women,
(c) Working women as better wives better mothers and managers of home

2. *Employment*

To study the attitudes of working women towards:

(a) Reasons for taking up employment
(b) Sources of motivation for employment,

(c) Continuing in job after marriage
(d) Employment versus marriage

3. Marriage

To find out whether there is any change in the attitudes of the working women with regard to:

(a) Divorce
(b) Mate choice
(c) Love marriage versus arranged marriage
(d) Dowry
(e) Widow remarriage
(f) Family planning

4. Family

To examine the changing views of working women about

(a) Reasons for staying in joint family
(b) Reasons for staying in nuclear family
(c) Interaction between joint and nuclear familiar

II. To find out the changing status and role of working women in relation to family members:

(a) To analyse the position as perceived by the respondents in relation to husband and parents- in- law
(b) To know if the working women have any freedom to buy
(c) To know whether or not the working women are involved in decision making regarding family matters,
(d) To find out if the family members shared domestic chores of the family, and
(e) To analyse whether the working women faced any

problems of adjustment with the husband and parents-in-law

III. To study if the working women are accorded their due status and role in office more specifically, it was intended to find out

(a) The interpersonal relations (trust and confidence) with men and women colleagues,

(b) How the working women perceived their efficiency in office in relation to men

(c) To know the attitude of male workers – cooperative, or non-cooperative or uncooperative towards female workers.

(d) To study the attitudes of office staff – superiors, colleagues and subordinates towards working women,

(e) To analyse if the working women took active part in office functions. And,

(f) To understand the attitudes of working women towards workers union with regard to membership and participation in union activities like submission of memorandums taking out processions and going our hunger strikes.

REVIEW OF LITERATURE

A review of available literature as related to the subject is an important and integral part of any research project. A critical survey of the literature on the subject will help in knowing the aims and objectives; methodology; and findings of theses and projects in the past. A review of literature thus helps in identifying the research gaps of a subject and need for the present study.

Promilla Kapur's studies on working women occupy an important place among the studies conducted on the subject.

In her thesis "Marriage and Working Women" (1970), she proposed to find out how successfully the educated working wives had been able to achieve and maintain harmony and happiness in their married and family life. In other words, the study sought to examine how far, in spite of the newly imposed responsibilities of their jobs, Indian working wives had been able to make adjustments in their married and family life.

The study was conducted in Delhi on a sample of 300 major occupational categories, namely, teachers, office workers, and doctors, each category consisting of 100 women. The study concluded that employment of a married woman did not affect her marital adjustment adversely.

Khanna and Varghese (1978) made a broad survey of women in India. The purpose of the investigation was to study the status of women and their role in the family and society in general. A sample of 1000 women, drawn from Calcutta, Cuttack, Gauhati, Darjeeling, Ranchi, Allahabad, Lucknow, Delhi, Ahmedabad, Bombay, Nagpur, Chennai, Bangalore, Trivandrum and Kottayam, was studied. The majority of the women were housewives and only 20 per cent of them were working. The study has revealed that there was a significant change in the women's attitudes towards inter-caste marriage, divorce, widow remarriage, family planning, co-education, sex education and girl's education because of increased education and economic development (p. 195). The study is a broad survey of changing status of women in modern India. The findings of the study are categorical and broad but not authentic, as the study is not based on any sound theory and methodology.

Rama Mehta (1970) made a study of educated Hindu elite women in the early '50s. The objective of the thesis was to find out to what extent traditional customs and values still operated in Indian society. To be specific, it tried to gauge the influence of Western education on them, identify the spheres in which it was effective and whether its impact resulted in merely a superficial limitation of western ways of living or whether it went deeper and changed the traditional value system and led to an assimilation of western ways and modes of thought. The sample consisted of 50 graduate and post-graduate young and married women drawn from different castes and from different provinces in India. The study was a very broad survey of the attitudes and values of a few selected Hindu women. The study was not conducted with reference to any theoretical framework. Methodologically, the study was very weak. The sample of 50 respondents spread all over India cannot be taken to warrant its representativeness. Of course, one can understand the difficulties a researcher had to encounter in the early fifties.

The study has broadly given some clues about changes taking place in the attitudes and values of educated women in spite of all its defects. The study is a pioneering work in the sense that it was undertaken in the early '50s.

C.A. Hate's (1969) study "Changing status of Women" was one of the earliest sociological works on working women. Middle-class women from four corporate cities of Maharashtra—Bombay, Poona, Nagpur and Solapur—were selected for the study.

The objective of the study was to find out how far the middle class woman was able to have added stature to her personality along with the old biological roles in the post-independence period. Samples from educated earning women, in contrast to a few non-earning women in relation to the family with a middle class background were chosen for the study. However, the study was not rigorous from the theoretical and methodological points of view. For example, what was the total population of the working and non-working women? How was the sample selected? Even the findings are not clear.

Mamata Agarwal (1986) made a study of "Education and Modernisation". In the study under reference an attempt was made to find out the impact of education as a modernizing force on women. It was proposed to compare the social and cultural values of educated Hindu and Muslim women with those of their uneducated counterparts so as to find out how far education had been successful in modernising the women belonging to different religious groups.

The study was conducted on a sample of 300 women of different age groups belonging to both the Hindu and Muslim communities residing in suburban areas of Delhi. But the study does not specify the total population of the educated and uneducated, Hindu and Muslim women in the universe. It was also not clear how the sample of 300 respondents was selected. Methodologically, the study is very weak. The study revealed that education made a significant change in the attitudes and values of women. But the changes were more in the case of Hindu women than Muslim.

In his paper, Murickan (1977) has reported the findings of several studies, which were conducted in three metropolitan centres of Kerala. What emerged most strikingly was the progress of formal education among women and the impact which education and urbanisation, among other variables, had made on the values and attitudes of the younger generation of women. Education appears to be of pivotal importance not only because in this case it had enabled the women to become economically independent but also because through it they had acquired the self-confidence necessary to assert their dignity and human rights. Nevertheless, the fact remains that the mass of women in Kerala lags far behind their middle-class sisters in the urban centres of Kerala. Most women in Kerala continue to live under male dominance and to be hampered by traditional cultural and religious taboos. Education by itself is not enough to liberate women. Only a strong mass-based movement organised by enlightened female leadership will be able to provide women with freedom and equality to work in partnership with men for their mutual development.

A. Ramanamma (1979) made a study of "Graduate Employed Women in an Urban Setting". The main objective of the study was to assess.

1. The structural changes brought about in various institutions due to the changing positions of women arising out of their education and employment, and
2. The problems of employed women in Indian society and the significance of these problems for the society at large.

The study sought to examine the changes occurring in the family, friendship and marriage patterns due to education and employment in urban women. The study was done in Poona city and its suburbs. A list of employed women working in various offices, schools etc in the Poona city and its suburbs was prepared. A sample of 505 educated women from six different occupations was chosen. The data were obtained mainly by administering an anonymous questionnaire to the women. The study broadly indicated that changes were occurring in the educated and employed women. However, the study suffered from many defects.

1. The study was not clear about its sample-size and selection methods. For example, what was the total population of educated working women in Poona city and its suburbs and how was the sample of 505 respondents selected?

2. The sample included both married and unmarried respondents. But most questions were addressed commonly without any distinction being made between married and unmarried respondents.
3. The issues connected with employed women were mainly centered in the family and work place. The study has not dealt with the issues exhaustively.

Vanita Srivastava (1978) undertook a study of "Employment of Educated Married Women in India". The study intended to seek answers to two main questions:

1. What were the reasons why some women worked? and
2. How did participation in gainful employment affect the behaviour pattern and life style of the women?

To be specific, the above investigation was conducted mainly to find out the causes and consequences associated with employed educated married women vis-à-vis non-working women. Out of 456 married educated working women from various Government Offices, P.G. Institute of Medical Education and Research, Panjab University, women's colleges and schools, a sample of 150 was selected. The method followed in selecting non-working women was as follows.

Each of the working women interviewed was asked to give three names of the non-working wives of her husband's colleagues. Out of such non-working women or wives, a sample of 150 was selected for study. However, it is not clear what the total population of non-working women was and how the sample of 150 was selected.

The study has revealed that the working women differed from the non-working women with regard to fertility, family size and socialisation of children. However, the working women could not devote time and energy to the management of home and development of the children, compared to non-working women. It means employment has impaired the performance of a women's basic roles as wife and mother. Working women, compared to non-working ones, depended on labour-saving devices and domestic servants or relatives. An important finding of the study was that the role of working women did not undergo any significant change as a consequence of the economic contribution that they made towards the family kitty.

M. Indiradevi (1987) made a study of "Women's Education Employment: Family Living". The main purpose of the study was to examine the significance of education and employment in promoting egalitarian relationships between husbands and wives. The sample was selected from a census conducted by the investigator. A sample of 80 families, drawn from each of the two population groups, one representing families with educated wives only and the other consisting of both educated and employed wives, was selected. But it is not clear what the universe was and what the total population of educated women and educated employed women was. The unit of study was the family. Thus, a total of 160 families representing diverse socio-economic and cultural groups with varying educational backgrounds were considered. A sample of 160 is a very small number when there is a comparison of two categories of sub-samples.

Blumberg and Dawarki (1980) conducted their study on educated women of Bangalore city in phases. The main focus of their study was to examine the intermeshing of education and marriage systems as they affected the life of their respondents. The study revealed that educated women were finding it very difficult to work, especially after marriage, as they had no place to leave their kids and had to have trustworthy servants. Surprisingly, the authors observed that most women behaved in a way that suggested that their broader experience made them more tolerant in their relationship with their in-laws. Finally, the authors concluded that women who tried to meet the traditional role obligations of the Indian wife and mother and also spent many hours away from home in paid employment, were experiencing a "role overload" or "a double day". The combination of twin roles, where modern technology had not yet arrived to eliminate household drudgery, easily created strain.

Mohini Sethi (1976) undertook a study of "Modernisation of Working Women in Developing Societies". The purpose of the analytical study was to observe the trends in the cognitive structure, which one would expect from the modernisation process in a particular section of the women population. Thus, it was assumed that urbanisation, education and employment would bring about changes in the attitudes and beliefs of women in respect of equality, individuality and independence; to be specific, the study concerned itself with the attitudes and beliefs of women in two modernising societies-India and Turkey. In other words, the study tried to describe how the changed attitudes of women were linked with the modernisation of societies.

The universe of the research covered women working in central or state government in Ankara (Turkey) and Chandigad (India) in non-manual service occupations such as clerical, executive, managerial and professional. A sample of 120 respondents from Chandigadh and 108 from Ankara was selected. The study has broadly indicated that modernisation in the form of education and employment has brought about changes in the attitudes of working women towards equality and independence. However, the study suffers from many shortcomings. The sample is too small to be used for any worthwhile research. The findings are based on superficial responses of the respondents.

Anita Sharma (1990) conducted an empirical study of 200 working women of Delhi falling under different categories of professions. The basic objective was to evaluate the position of working women in India in the light of modernisation. The study has revealed that having education and employment to their credit made the working women have a different view about the existing society. It was found that a majority of the women after completing their education developed a tendency to seek a job even in the male-dominated occupational fields. With the growing economic independence, a sense of self-competence and independent existence among women started increasing. The women's interaction with the outside world developed in them a social skill, which has in due course been useful in influencing the family members.

K.N. Jha (1985), through his study of the college and university lady teachers residing and working in Patna, has made an attempt to find out the impact of modernisation on working women. It has been found that a rational and modern outlook is becoming increasingly apparent among such women. Their approach towards marriage, interpersonal relationships in the family and kinship network are changing, too. The women were found to be changing in their habits, manners and ways of life, which are now much different from the traditional patterns.

A study entitled "Women and Modern Occupations in India" was undertaken by Kumud Ranjan (1993). The aim of the study was to know if there was any relationship between the socio-economic status of the women's family and their educational achievements, as also their recruitment in modern occupations. Thus, in the study an attempt was made to find out how parental family influenced the educational attainment and career choice of women, as also to explore husband-wife congruency status, which affected both the performance of work role and domestic roles of the working women (P. 27).

The universe of the present study consisted of women working in Government Offices or following independent professions in the two cities of Uttar Pradesh, Allahabad and Varanasi.

A sample of 300 (100 from each city) drawn from different occupations was selected. But it is not clear what was the total number of women working in jobs and of those pursuing independent professions. It appears that the sampling design was not properly worked out. According to the findings, educated working women are becoming courageous, bold and self-assertive. Most of the household chores are assigned to servants. But husbands never engaged in domestic chores. On the whole it appears that educated working women were acquiring greater freedom and independence at the hands of their husbands, parents or parents-in-law.

A study was undertaken by Shashi Jain (1988) on the "Status and Role Perception of Middle Class Women". The study was viewed from the perspective of Middle Class women, and had a reference to the wider process of social change in the country. The study was aimed at finding out what changes in the status-role sets of women have occurred and what conflicts and restraints, as issues of adjustment, have been introduced in her status and role under the overall process of change. The study, based as it was on the educated Hindu Middle Class Women of the two important cities of UP, represented a cultural cross-section of the state. The study was based on a sample of 200 working and 200 non-working women.

An important study was conducted by M. Hanumantha Rao (1990) on "Employment of the Wife and Husband's Participation in House-work". The study attempted to understand the areas of housework in which the husbands of the working women participated. The study also aimed at exploring the relationship between certain socio-economic, demographic, family-structural and, attitudinal variables, and the husbands' participation in housework.

The sample consisted of 186 women working in white collar jobs in Tirupathi. The findings of the study have questioned the contention that employment of women compels their husbands to extend help in shouldering domestic duties.

M.R. Wood (1975) made an in-depth study of middle class women in urban Gujarat. The aim of the study was to analyse how educated and employed middle class Gujarati women responded to the new challenges of modernisation. To assess patterns of familial behaviour and attitude among urban middle-class women, a survey of thirty-two respondents was conducted in Ahmedabad in 1968-79. The selection of respondents was made in a non-random fashion. The main conclusion of the study was that employed women tended to make love marriages, have small families and to relate to members of their households in an egalitarian manner in contrast to their non-employed counterparts. In sum, according to the author, employment might foster in women a dynamic and pragmatic approach to life, an individualistic view of life, and cosmopolitan orientation attitudes which are manifested in the working women's patterns of family life and in their changing familial roles.

The findings of the study were based on a very small sample. The sampling method was also defective. It is true that there are changes visible in the attitudes and values of educated working women, but the findings of the study with regard to "love marriage" and egalitarian relations with members of the household are highly vague and ambiguous.

Inder Kaur (1983) studied "Status of Hindu women in India". The aim in this enquiry was to find out the values, which were shaping the outlook of the Hindu women who had received the benefit of modern education and who had been exposed to modern influences in an urban setting. A sample of 300 graduate women residing in Gorakhpur city was selected for the study. The findings show that changes in the values of middle class women were taking place with regard to choice of mates, dowry, family, education etc. However, it is felt that the findings needed more rigorous examination. For example, do educated women really protest against the practice of dowry?

K. Lalithadevi (1982) conducted a systematic study of the "Status and Employment of Women in India". The aim of the study was to establish the primacy of employment over other factors such as age, education, family type, and place of residence and level of income, in enhancing the social status of women in society. The major hypothesis put forward in the study was that employment was significantly related to raising a woman's status in society. A sample of 300 working women and 100 non-working women was selected for the interview. The study has concluded that employment did enhance women's status in many walks of life.

V.V. Prakash Rao and V. Nandini Rao (1982) compiled nine research papers that were written over a period of seven years on the basis of data collected at different periods: 1967, 1973 and 1975. The book dealt with the following topics:

1. Arranged marriage.
2. Ideal age of marriage
3. The dowry system
4. Sex and dowry
5. Choice of the family system
6. The status of Women
7. The Employed mother

8. Employed and Non-Employed mothers.
9. Marriage and the family in India.

By and large, the study has revealed that employment has introduced positive changes in the role and status of working women.

A study of unmarried working women by Manjula (1990) was unique in itself. The purpose of the study was to analyse the orientation of unmarried educated working women towards various aspects of marriage and career. The study also aimed at exploring the views these women had towards related issues such as education of females, the factors and forces promoting new alternatives for women and of motivation for choosing a new style of life. The author used personal and familial characteristics as the means for approaching these objectives. The study raised the following research questions:

1. Was there any fundamental change in the level of consciousness among women as regard their position, which was based on gender division of labour after they got the new educational opportunities? Or was there not?
2. How did the unmarried working women view their career-oriented role system and life-style?
3. What was the extent of synthesis and contradiction between the values, norms and practices related with the marriage-oriented traditional role complexe and those of the career-oriented modern role system in the perception of the educated unmarried working women?

The study was undertaken in Varanasi, U. P. A sample of 120 unmarried college teachers was selected for the study. A majority of the respondents came from the Hindu upper caste and nuclear families living in urban areas. The findings are as follows:

Higher education was perceived by unmarried educated working women more as an instrument of personality development and economic independence than as a passport for marriage.

The respondents believed that career was as important as marriage. So much so that they were not prepared to sacrifice career for marriage and family.

Krishna Chakravorthi (1978) conducted a sociological enquiry into the Conflicting Worlds of Working Mothers. The aim of the study was to explore the factors that created a role conflict in working mothers. The hypothesis was that combining childcare and housekeeper roles with that of provider will create feelings of guilt, anxiety, strain and tensions among working mothers themselves.

A sample of 161 working mothers from the middle class category of the city of Culcutta, who had children and husbands economically active, and who were drawn from four major occupational categories viz school and college teachers, gazetted and non-gazetted officer-workers, doctors and nurses employed in Govt. hospitals.

The finding is that employment of woman does affect the smooth discharge of motherly responsibilities.

Napasri Kraisoneswadi (1989) made a study of Women Executives: A Sociological Study in Role Effectiveness. The study was designed to seek answers to three main questions.

1. In which way and to what extent did private and public sectors perceive the structure of their work organization differently?

2. What were the desirable traits and behaviour patterns of the successful women executives in Thailand? and
3. What was the extent of role effectiveness of the women executives in their society?

A sample of 200 women executives was studied in the city of Bangkok. The sample was selected, based on a quasi-random sampling technique. The study has revealed that women executives played their role much better than expected.

Usha Talwar (1984) in her thesis 'Social Profile of Working Women' presented a comprehensive account of the social profile of working women. To be specific, the main objectives of the study were:

1. To specify the social characteristics of working women.
2. To identify the reasons for the employment.
3. To examine the division of labour in the family.
4. To analyse the role of working women in decision-making.
5. To study the effects on Children.
6. To understand the pattern of marital interaction.
7. To inquire in to the work conditions of the working women.
8. To comprehend the pattern of community role and leisure time activities and,
9. To assess the opinions and attitudes of the working women.

The study was conducted in Jodhpur City of Rajasthan. It was based on the responses of 400 working and 400 non-working women. The working women were selected randomly from a population of working women of the city. The non-working women were selected through a procedure known as "ecological sampling".

The study suffers from many shortcomings. The phrase "working woman" is not defined clearly. The author has mixed up women working in unorganized and organised sectors. Such a study of petty traders and jobholders does not help in arriving at valid findings.

A review of the literature on working women has revealed the following points.

1. The sample size of most studies in relation to the total population in the universe is very small.
2. Many studies have not adopted appropriate methods of sample selection.
3. Most studies on working women are mere repetitions without substantial differences in the content and methodology.
4. Most studies have not defined, clearly, concepts like education, employment, working woman etc.

THEORETICAL PERSPECTIVE: EDUCATION, EMPLOYMENT AND STATUS OF WOMEN

This section deals with the role of education and employment in bringing about changes in the status and role of Indian Women in the context of the emerging phenomenon of modernisation.

Meaning of Modernisation

The concept of modernisation is of recent origin. It came into being with the advent of science and technology, democracy, secularism and the concept of the welfare state. With the opportunity of modern education throne open by the colonial powers to the relatively backward societies of the erstwhile colonies, forces of modernisation were released. And gradually these societies were moving towards modernity, and mobility, in the process, the values that modernity represents. Modernisation refers to the scientific temper, religious tolerance, cosmopolitanism, welfarism, equality, social justice and democracy. It was earlier held that traditional societies and cultures, being highly conservative, would not respond positively to the demands of modernisation. Scholars like Milton Singer (1956, 1958, 1968), Rudolph and Rudolph (1967) and Gould (1963) posited that traditional societies can become modern by adopting and assimilating modern values like equality, secularism, without totally discarding their fundamental social value orientations. Modernisation aims at bringing about a harmonious adjustment between tradition and modernity by undergoing selective changes. It does not signify the undoing of an older tradition. Only it tries to discard outdated and useless ways of thinking and living by interpreting tradition in the light of modern values as stated above. According to this theory, employment of women can bring about changes in their status and enable them to play a more positive and constructive role in the family and the society, although it may take time. Working women may become modern in certain aspects of life but remain traditional in certain other aspects. For example, a working woman may assert her rights but wish to accept the superiority of the husband and of other older members of the family. Available research has shown that modernisation in traditional societies is not a smooth process. In the initial stages at least it brings in its train problems of conflict, discord and mal- adjustment. The degree and intensity of conflict varies from society to society.

In the following pages an attempt is made to analyse the part played by education and employment of women in bringing about changes in their role and status, against the background of Indian Institutions of marriage, family etc.

Education and Status of Women

The educational system is one of the basic institutions

through which the social and cultural heritage of the society is transmitted from one generation to another. It is, as Emile Durkheim (1956) observed, above all the means by which society perpetually recreates the conditions of its very existence. According to Harbison and Myers (1964:181), education is the key that unlocks the door to modernisation. Broadly speaking, education through reading, writing, and numeracy underlines an ability to think, grasp and comprehend and analyse the happenings of life. It enlarges one's vision by exposing them to the external world.

Higher education kindles new aspirations and ambitions and develops a sense of self-respect and individuality. It makes people mobile. Higher education also develops values of scientific temper, tolerance, empathy and national consciousness.

Education, especially professional and technical, graduate and post-graduate, has come to be linked with employment. Occupations at different levels require different types and levels of education: graduating as a minimum level of education, appearing for competitive examinations.

A developing economy requires a literate population, a well-trained group of executives, administrators and professionals who are capable of running the government; and introducing modern methods and techniques. In modern India, education in terms of certificates, diplomas and degrees have been a necessary requirement for men and women to secure white-collar jobs. Thus, education in modern society has become a central determinant of the individual's life chances, that is his/her opportunities for employment, earning and status (Chinoy, 1967:392).

The advent of independence ushered in a new era with respect to women's education. With the introduction of formal education and its expansion, with a special emphasis on the provision for women's education, a large number of girls began to enroll themselves in schools and colleges. With the growth of education among women, they are more and more exposed to the external world of science and technology, public life, mass media, politics etc. Consequently significant changes have taken place in their ways of thinking, of attitudes and values. Education has enabled them to develop their own identity, autonomy and independence. There is a change also in the perception of their role and status. Educated women, especially in urban areas, are growing aware of the rights and privileges, which exist in law and to which they are entitled. Ross (1961) reported that a majority of girl students wanted greater freedom and independence and aspired for jobs and careers. According to Hotler (1971:11) increased higher education for women is the royal road that leads to changes in woman power and self-respect. Educated women in India are today more conscious of their rights, and look to the future with more confidence for better adjustment with husbands, families and society based on mutual understanding rather than simply on dominance over them. It is being increasingly documented that educated women have grown more aware of themselves and about the world and want to play a more constructive role in society. Education, however, cannot transform Indian values into western. On the contrary, education can play the role of an agent of modernisation in strengthening and promoting traditional values and practices. Modern education has had a deep impact on women's outlook. Values, which they cherished under the influence of tradition, are undergoing a radical transformation. In fact, a new concept of womanhood is gradually emerging in India which is often at odds with the traditional concept of Indian woman as a devout wife confined to the hearth and home. Other studies (Vohra and Sen: 1985; Ross, 1961) have reported that education has helped to improve the girls' marriage prospects.

Employment and Status of Women

With the advent of industrialisation, urbanisation, mechanisation, formal education and growth and expansion of administrative structures and the mass media, a large number of white-collar jobs have become available for both men and women. Education, especially higher education, has promoted employment aspirations in women. A change in the means of production and structure of economy have offered a greater role for women in the productive function. Transformation in the gender-based occupational structure has provided a vast scope for women's employment in modern India. According to Hotler (1971) the needs of the economic system with respect to labour and consumption are seen as promoting a change from traditional sex roles to quasi egalitarianism. Klein (1968:27) has pointed out that women, especially educated ones, in the modern industrialised society have become a part and parcel of manpower resource.

Employment in general, and for women in particular, plays a great role as anagent of social change. In terms of salary it is a definite source of income. It also means a definite position in the hierarchy of the office, which enables women to command respect and honor. Besides, employment provides opportunities for social interaction with a large number of men and women. In short, employment introduces many changes in the personality, role and status of women. It provides power, prestige and honor. With employment, a new identity, self-image of womanhood are developing in women. To conclude, education and employment will play a great role in modernising women's perception of themselves, their role and status.

STATUS AND ROLE: A CONCEPTUAL ANALYSIS

A study of the status and role of working women requires an exhaustive conceptual analysis of the terms 'status' and 'role'.

At the outset it should be stressed that status and role constitute a composite concept. They carry both a narrower and a broader meaning. Status and role constitute a composite of interdependent concepts. The meaning of each term can be understood in relation to the other. Broadly speaking, human society can be defined as an organization of statuses and roles. They reflect the system of social stratification and social ideology. It is through status and role that individuals and groups are integrated with society. A study of the concepts of status and role will provide an indispensable starting point for the analysis of social structure.

Meaning of Status

Status is a term used to designate the comparative degrees of prestige, deference, or respect accorded to persons in society. Status refers to rights, power, authority and privileges accorded to persons and groups in society. According to MacIver(1988), "status is the social position that determines for its possessor, apart from his personal attribute of social services, a degree of respect, prestige and influence". The definition points out that status as position has its own values, norms and prestige, irrespective of the incumbent's personal merit. K. Davis (1958) makes a distinction between social status and official status or what is popularly called ascribed status and achieved status. He says that social status is a position in the general institutional system, recognised and supported by the entire society. It is spontaneously evolved rather than deliberately created and rooted in the folkways and mores. Official status, on the other hand, would designate a position in a deliberately created organisation, governed by a specific and limited group, more generally achieved and ascribed.

Examples of social status are father, mother, husband, wife, brothers, and sisters. Such positions are called ascribed statuses. Such statuses derive their importance and strength from tradition, ideology and values. Examples of official status are Officer, supervisor, clerk, peon, teacher, constable etc. The term 'social status' connotes a broader meaning than 'official status'. The former is rooted in society, culture and ideology, whereas the latter is rooted in formal organisation. An officer may command respect in his office but not necessarily in society. Although the two forms of status are theoretically different from each other, for all practical purposes, they cannot be separated from each other.

As we have stated earlier the concept of status is much broader than what it is generally understood to be; it involves a good deal of interpersonal relationship between individuals and groups, what is socially or officially accorded is not perceived. In other words, an individual's status is always dependent to a great extent on how others or status- set members perceive and value him / her, on the amount of prestige they are willing to according to him / her. The amount of status possessed by an individual will be determined by the extent to which he/ she is able to influence others, to make his/her own decisions, and expect differences from others

As we stated earlier, the term status can also be defined from a broader point of view. It can be defined in relation to statuses held by others in the system. An individual's status is not a single status, but a multidimensional structure. That means every status has related statuses. This is called 'status-set'. For example, a person in the family, is related as a father to his children, as a husband to his wife, as a brother to his brothers. Similarly, a principal of a college is related to his staff, both teaching and non-teaching, students, management (if it is aided). A person in a given status has to interact with other related statuses. Thus every status is a cluster of statuses.

Meaning of Role

'Role' and 'status' are two sides of the same coin. Ralph

Linton (1936) defines roles in terms of actions that are performed by an individual to validate his occupancy of a position. According to K. Davis (1958) a role is the manner in which a person actually carries out the requirement of his position. It is the function of status. Role is the expected pattern of behaviour in relation to a status. For example, a mother has a role to play with regard to her children in the family. The term "role" refers to one's duties, responsibilities and obligations towards certain needs and expectations.

Role-Set: Like status, the role is also a multidimensional concept. The meaning of role can be understood when its related roles are taken into account. A woman plays the role of wife, mother and daughter-in-law. When a woman is married into a family, she enters the family not only as wife, but also as a daughter-in-law, sister-in-law etc. A person in a family or office has to play a number of related roles simultaneously. The concept of role-set suggests the complex nature of role and recognizes that a given status generates more than one role. Merton (1968) introduced the concept of role-set. He said a single status, such as husband, involves an array of associated roles. When one enters a new status one usually acquires not a unitary role but a role-set, because one must meet the expectations of a number of different people. The term 'role-set' is used to indicate that a status may have not just a single role, but also a number of associated roles which function together (Merton, 1957). Status and role are comprehensive concepts. Any change in status provided through education, employment, social legislation will bring about changes in roles. Similarly any changes in roles brought about by perception of new laws enacted to protect women against exploitation etc. will bring about changes in the status.

Ascribed and Achieved Status

When we speak of the status and role of working women, the terms are used in the sense of social status and official position, as pointed out by Davis. Broadly speaking, there are two types of statuses as we noted before ascribed and achieved. According to Linton, (1936) ascribed statuses are assigned to individuals without reference to their innate differences or abilities. They can be predicted and trained for from the moment of birth. Age, sex, caste, religion, kinship etc. may be given as examples. Older people are superior to youngsters. Parents are superior to children, and men are superior to women.

The second type of status is achieved. According to Linton, achieved statuses are those requiring special qualities, although they are not necessarily limited to these. Achieved statuses are not assigned to persons by birth. They are left out to be filled through competition and individual effort. Among the commonly recognised achieved statuses are those depending on education, occupation, income, and political clout.

Although we have given the meaning of status and role purely from the academic point of view, there exists a good deal of ambiguity and confusion about their meaning in practical life. For example, the mother-in-law, by virtue of her ascribed status, is superior to the daughter-in-law. The relationship between the two is one of super-ordination and subordination. This relationship can work well as far as both function in their ascribed status. However, if the daughter-in-law has a certain level of achieved status in terms of education and occupation, she has a combination of two types of statuses and roles; ascribed and achieved. Education and occupation will give a new boost to her status and role. But the mother-in-law, who has only ascribed status, will still behave in her traditional manner of ordering, supervising and controlling, which may upset the employed daughter-in-law. Such mutually contradictory or confusing situations may lead to role conflict in the family.

The Concept of Status of Woman

Any attempt to define the status of woman, in the context of democracy, welfarism and modernisation, should take into account their strengths and weaknesses — social, economic, religious and physical.

Women compared to men, are considered weak. By nature, women suffer from certain disabilities and handicaps, which to a great extent affect their status and role in society. Studies tend to support the notion that women are physically the weaker sex, because they have a more passive sex and social role (Overstreet, 1963, Maccoby, 1961). For example, women are vulnerable during menstrual periods and pregnancy. Besides, bearing and rearing functions are assigned by nature to women. Taking advantage of women's handicaps and disabilities, men have always exploited by subjecting them to physical and sexual assaults, torture, harassment, molestation and rape. Malinowski (1949) has pointed out that a correct definition of the status of woman can be given only after taking into consideration all mutual duties between the sexes, and the safeguards provided for the protection of each sex against the high-handedness of the other. Lowie (1913) has shown that status may mean four different things, all the four of which may not, however, be found to exist together anywhere. Thus actual treatment, legal status, opportunities for social participation and the character and extent of work, all determine, each in a specific sense and manner, the status of woman in a society. Dixon (1978:6) defines the status of woman as the degree of woman's access to, and control of, material resources (including food, income, land and other forms of wealth) and her access to social resources (including knowledge, power and prestige) within the family, in the community and in the society at large.

The status of the working woman in the present study, both in the family and in the office, is understood as:

1. Right of empowerment, authority to decide for one's life
2. Opportunities to develop her social self
3. Sharing of domestic responsibilities by other members, including husband
4. Freedom accorded for participation in social and public activities
5. The degree of deferential treatment given
6. Provision for protection of women from their exploitation, harassment and disabilities.

Mukherjee (1975) proposes an operational definition of "Status of Woman": By status of woman we mean a set of expectations regarding the attributes pertaining to the duties and responsibilities of women in their roles as a daughter, wife, mother, worker, head of the household, etc and the actions, rewards or rights which they expect from others in these positions, as well as others' perception of the actual rewards accompanying these positions.

The status of woman may be defined as the total configuration of the attributes associated with various positions which a woman may occupy in the society at a given point of time and the perception of these attributes by the occupant of the position as well as by others, each weighing the attributes according to his or her cultural centrality and individual frame of reference.

A multifaceted conception of the status of woman should then mean "The conjunction of rights and duties" as reflected in the several roles of women as mothers, as wives, as sisters or daughters, as wage earners etc. , their position in family decision-making, and the degree of control over their own lives; in fact their perception of differential privileges, prerogatives and decision-making power etc. (Mukharjee, 1975).

Meaning of Concepts

In the following paragraphs it is intended to explain the meaning of the terms used in the study.

Work or Employment

In the present study terms like 'work' and 'employment' are used interchangeably. Work or employment may be broadly defined as labour participation in gainful activities. The NSSO defines gainful activity as value to the national product. The NSSO further adds that gainful activity normally results in production of goods and services for exchange and that the activities in agriculture in which a part or whole of the agricultural production is used for own consumption and does not go for sale are considered gainful.

The Census of India defines "work" as participation in any economically productive activity. In its opinion an adult woman who is engaged in household duties, but doing no other productive work to augment the family's resources should not be considered as working i. e. , unless she works for wages or sales.

Work may be viewed either as productive activity for household use or for exchange. The work organisation divides society into those who perform work for themselves and those for whom others work. Work means wage-earning.

The jobs women perform to support their families do not always or necessarily bring in money or returns. The work done by women at home has, as is often termed by economists, "use value" rather than "exchange value". A woman may engage in household labour. But this is always treated as non-productive labour. Market labour is said to be the only productive labour as it has exchange value.

Educated and Employed Woman

"Educated woman" and "employed Woman" are used in different senses by researchers.

Educated Woman

To study the impact of education on the role and status, education is operationalised without sound theoretical justifications. For example Agarwal (1986:114) and Lalitha Devi (1982:33) used S.S.L.C. as the minimum to be considered as "educated". But taking into account the present standard of education, S.S.L.C. does not equip the person with any significant ability to set in motion the process of modernisation. Education in terms of college education can be thought of as an agent of modernisation. Therefore, in our study, a minimum of graduation is considered to be important in bringing about changes in the role and status of the woman.

Employed Woman

Like the phrase "educated woman", the phrase "employed woman" is also not operationalised with appropriate basics. According to Usha Talwar (1984) a working woman is that woman who is earning full or part of her livelihood by engaging herself in any occupation or work for pay or profit. But women who are self-employed or are working on contract basis cannot have serious problems of adjustment with the role as wife and mother.

In our study 'working' or 'employed' woman is defined as one who is gainfully employed by Government or Semi-Government agencies like Schools, Colleges, and University, Government Hospital, Government Offices etc. and whose services have been approved and regularised by the office or department concerned.

2

Universe and Methodology

The Field of Study: Gulbarga City

The aim of this chapter is to provide a brief picture of the historical, socio-economic and educational background of Gulbarga City with the main focus on developing aspects of women.

1. Location and History

Gulbarga is located in the Northern region of Karnataka state. It lay on the Deccan Plateace and is made up of Deccan Trap and sedimentary rock formations. Gulbarga city is a center of religious importance and pilgrimage. It is an abode of two great 14th century saints: 1) Kwaja Bande Nawaz, and, 2) Sharanbasaveswhwar.

2. *Gulbarga: A developing City*

Before Independence, Gulbarga district was part of the erstwhile Hyderabad state. On the 17th sept. , 1948, Gulbarga, along with Bidar and Raichur, became part of the present Karnataka State (the then Mysore State). Gulbarga has been classified as a backward city-socially, economically and educationally. However, in the last five decades there is considerable progress in all walks of life.

According to 1991 census, the total population of the city was 523944, out of which 272398 and 251546 were men and women, respectively. Of the total, 213024 and 310920 constituted rural and urban population, respectively. According to Gulbarga District at a Glance-1996-97, the total literacy rate of the city was 57. 33 percent. Out of which literacy rate for men and women was 70. 12 and 43. 41, respectively. There is tremendous improvement in the number of schools and colleges. According to Gulbarga District at a Glance-1996-97, there were 370 primary schools, 141 high schools; 15 independent junior colleges; 24 non-professional colleges; 2 engineering colleges; 5 polytechnic colleges and; 1 medical college. In 1973, a university has been established. In the last five decades educated women have taken to white-collar jobs. Women are also responding favourably to self-employment schemes such as PMRY. In short, Gulbarga is a developing city with better opportunities for higher education and white-collar jobs.

Research Design

The universe of the study was Gulbarga City in Karnataka. Graduate women working in the various offices, educational institutions, banks located in Gulbarga city constituted the respondents.

Preparation of Sample Frame

The first problem we encountered was identification of the sample unit and drawing up of the sample size. Since there was no up-to-date, reliable and readily available sampling frame or list of sample units for deciding the sample size and selecting the respondents, it was decided to hold a census of the working women in various offices, schools, colleges university, and banks located in Gulbarga city. A list of working women from all offices, schools, colleges, university and banks was obtained. The total number of working women was around 10,000. Again we contacted the offices concerned and inquired about educational qualifications. There were 5,000 graduate working women. On further inquiry it was found that a number of them were working on daily wage/

contract basis, as part-timers and stopgap appointees. All such temporary and unconfirmed working women were kept out of consideration for interview. A large number of graduate women who were working in private (i. e. unaided by state government) schools, colleges and hospitals were also not considered for the study.

Reasons for not considering Temporary or Unconfirmed Working Women

The reasons for not considering unconfirmed or temporary working women or those serving in private (unaided) institutions are as follows:

1. Services of temporary employees may be terminated as soon as the contract is over, or the staff on leave report back for duty. Obviously, such working women may keep on looking for jobs elsewhere or even decide not to seek employment in future.
2. It was also assumed that women working on temporary basis are not likely to develop stable attitudes, values, plans and goal of employment. Obviously, views of such employees should not have any decisive bearing on the findings of the study.

Sample Design

The sample design of any research project is very important. An appropriate sample design will ensure relatively more reliable findings, scientific statements and conclusions. A research design must address three things:

1.Where the sample is to be selected from

2.The process of selection and

3.The size of the sample

Selection of Sample

After a rigorous exercise of eliminating unrelated

respondents from the universe, there were 1600 working women eligible for the study at the time of the interview during 1997-98.

The Process of Selection of the Sample

It was decided to select the sample according to stratified systematic sampling method, as the population in the universe was diverse in its designations and length of service. In order to identify the respondents a simple questionnaire consisting of items like name, address of office and residence, telephone number, length of service and designation was administered to 1600 working women. A list containing the names, residential addresses and telephone numbers, designation and length of service of the interviewees was prepared.

Respondents were first arranged according to their designation. Then within their designation they were again arranged according to their length of service. Then every 4th respondent was selected for the study. The details are given in the following table.

Sampling Procedure

TABLE NO. II. 1

Population and Sample by Designation and Length of Service

Designation	*Length of Service*			
	0-5	*5-10*	*10-15*	*Total*
High	300(75)	200(50)	500(125)	1000(250)
Medium	100(25)	100(25)	200(50)	400(100)
Low	100(25)	50(12)	50(12)	200(50)
Total	500(125)	350(87)	750(185)	1600(400)

Note: Figures in brackets relate to the actual sample.

Sample Size

A sample size of 400 working women was decided for the study. A sample of 400 was thought enough for arriving at valid findings, keeping in view the time and financial constraints of a Ph. D. scholar. Although the actual sample size was 400, during our interview about 30 respondents were not ready for the interview. Another 20 evaded our questions. Finally the sample size was settled at 350.

Preparation of Interview Schedule

In conformity with the objectives of the study an interview schedule was prepared on issues such as

1. Social Background: individual and family
2. Attitudes towards education and employment
3. Attitude towards marriage and family
4. Role and status in the family and office

Pre-testing

The first draft of the schedule was pre-tested on 25 respondents from different occupations. Interview-ship of each respondent took at least one hour. Questions in the interview schedule were understood easily by the respondents. However, it was found that the respondents could not reveal their inner and true feelings through formal interviewing. Then it was decided to draw information through prolonged personal discussion. Accordingly the schedule was redrafted.

Methods of Data Collection

Data were collected through the interview method. Respondents were first contacted at their offices/institutions or residences and efforts were made to convince them of the objectives of the study. After securing their willingness and confidence, the schedule was administered to the respondents. In fact the schedule was used as a guide. A number of personal questions, whether directly or indirectly related to the main question, were asked through informal discussions, and answers were recorded. The aim was to get at the deeper feelings lying in the subconscious mind of the respondents. Views recorded through informal discussions have been used in the text wherever felt appropriate to support the main question. Interviewing women posed no problem since the investigator was herself one of their kind. Sometimes interviewees were contacted for the second time, if their responses were unclear. Unstructured information, collected through informal discussion during the interview, was carefully organised and written up later on. Data collection was completed in five months.

Nature of Study Design

The study is descriptive-cum-exploratory in nature. The study aimed at collecting not only structured responses, but also unstructured information about interpersonal relations between husband and wife, with mothers-in-law, daughters-in-law, brother-in-law and sister-in-law inner feelings about divorce and dowry etc.

Coding and Transfer of Data

In accordance with the aims and objectives of the research project a codebook was prepared. Experts in research methodology from the TISS, Mumbai were consulted. The interview schedules were checked up thoroughly by the investigator. Ambiguous and confusing responses were corrected and set right. Data were transferred from schedules to code sheets in about three months. The data were processed and tabulated at the Tata Institute of Social Sciences, Mumbai. A simple test like X^2 was applied to find out association between variables. This exercise took about three months.

3

The Changing Status of Woman Through the Ages in India

The aim of this chapter is:

1. To analyse the changing status of woman from ancient society to modern society, and
2. To describe the constitutional guarantees, social legislation, Government Policies, programmes and plans and, to examine their impact in raising the status of woman in modern India.

Status of Woman in Ancient India: Primitive and Vedic Society

The position of Hindu woman has been a subject of controversy. Conflicting, even contradictory, statements have been made about the status of woman in ancient India. In fact, a strange situation prevails in the Indian society. On the one hand, the women are placed on a pedestal and given a high place and, on the other, they are still being treated as second to men in all regards. We always hear of a woman being behind a successful man, never alongside of him. There is, thus, a contradictory attitude towards women as goddess and second-rate citizen, and sometimes even worse, a chattel (Sabbarwal, 1989). Most studies undertaken on the status of woman in ancient India have drawn their conclusions on the basis of classical books such as the Vedas, the Rigveda, the *Ramayana*, the *Mahabharatha* etc., without using a proper theoretical framework in relation to the position of woman. According to the studies of many ideologists and scholars of Hindu social organizations and woman's status in ancient India (Cormack, 1953; Prabhu, 1954; Altekar, 1962) in Vedic times, women were accorded equal status. There was no seclusion of women and they used to move about freely in society. In social and religious functions they occupied a prominent position. Women stood on a footing of absolute equality with men in the eyes of religion. They could perform sacrifices independent of men (Ghosh, 1989: 2). According to most authorities, women, by and large, enjoyed a high status equal to that of men at home and society till 300 BC.

On the other hand, Manu, the law-giver, has condemned women to the maximum, while praising them on some occasions. Manu says, "Women must always be honoured and respected by their fathers, brothers, husbands and brothers-in-law who desire their welfare. And, Manu says, where women are honoured, there the very gods are pleased, but where they are not honoured no sacred rite even could yield rewards. Here Manu has viewed woman as mother, sister, etc. who are revered by Hindus as symbols of Shakti. That Manu was right to that extent could be decided by taking into account the prevailing value system of a given society.

It appears Manu was unduly critical about women as individuals in society. Manu and other Smritikaras were not prepared to allow any kind of independent activity to women without consultation or permission of the male members of the family. She was not allowed to do anything independently even in her own home. Vatsayana, who generally holds more liberal views than Manu about the fair sex, also looks upon unrestrained independence for women with disapproval.

On other occasions, Manu has viewed the very nature of women with extreme contempt and prejudice. It is the nature of women to seduce men in this world, he says. He further adds that wise men should always guard themselves against the sexual desires of women. It is quite possible that Manu had come across a few examples where women might have exploited men. But it is wrong on the part of Manu to generalize about for the entire community of women.

Unfortunately, Manu has permitted men to go absolutely free and uncontrolled and to exploit women. They (men) are exempted from all kinds of moral codes. On the other hand, a study of *Dharmashastras* and *Manu Samhita* would give no definite indication of women's high status in Rigvedic society. The fact that the legendary Rama abandoned his wife when he suspected her character as soon as she was brought back from Lanka to Ayodhya and the legendary Droupadi was married to five brothers viz. Pandavas shows that women's status was not high as is generally believed.

Anthropologists have held that the status of woman in primitive society was relatively high. The tribal woman has a wide measure of freedom even by herself. She can visit her friends. She can dance and sing, especially before marriage, as she pleases. She could laugh and joke with men without reproach. Her freedom becomes naturally somewhat restricted after marriage, but even then she can be herself (Elvin in Jain). The high status of tribal women is measured by the fact that property was inherited by women and men worked under them. Women have the right to divorce and remarriage. It should be borne in mind that in the matriarchal system, marriage did not develop into a full-fledged institution. Marital relations between women and men were temporary. The husband was a casual visitor. For example, under Kulimusm in Bengal, where a Brahmin wife had to live with her parents and the husband, who was polygamous, visited the wives occasionally at their (wives) places, and children grew up in the house of their maternal uncle (Majumdar and Madan, 1980: 47). The Nairs being matrilineal and matrilocal, children born of Sambandham (temporary alliance) belonged to their mothers' Tarwad (family) and inherited property from the mother. The husband was a visitor to his wife's place, and children had no tie with him (Kapadia, 1958: 80). In a matriarchal system the woman was never assured marital security and stability. The responsibility of the women was to contract as many marital alliances with men of other tribes as possible and bear children, especially females, for the mother tribe. Women were used as machines for sexual satisfaction and to bear children. There were practices of women being sold in the market on bidding; wives were mortgaged, widows were inherited by creditors. Although property was inherited by women, men were vested with the power of controlling the family. According to Andre Beteille (1975:64), in practically all societies, whether patrilineal or matrilineal, women have, in fact, a lower status than men. In matrilineal societies property is transmitted through women, but this only means that it generally passes from mother's brother to sister's son. In most such cases the woman, instead of being under the control of her husband, is under her brother's control. Neither matriliny nor polyandry (where a single woman is at the same time married to several men) is a guarantee of the supremacy of women.

According to Neera Desai (1987: 193), although women in the matriarchal system enjoyed certain privileges, in practical life men were more powerful than women, "Contrary to this notion, one finds that although political power and social control is exercised by men they may be husbands or matrilineal kin. Although the line is continued through women, power rests with the men. The division of labour between the sexes emphasises differential rights and expectations. Men's superior physical qualities are recognized, war and politics is left to them. Rulers, chiefs, elders and managers of property, are men". It follows that women's high status in primitive society was symbolical in nature, while the men possessed all the powers.

Post-Vedic Society: Emergence of Patriarchal System

With the growth of socio-economic and politico-legal changes in society, the matriarchal society, with women as heads, could not withstand the challenges of the economy and invasion by other tribes. Temporary alliances and freedom of sex for women led to moral crises.

In view of the changing demands of an organized and settled life, men began to hold the reins of power and authority. A new philosophy of life with emphasis on stability of marriage and family bonds became the way of wife. Marriage became a sacred institution. Temporary sexual alliances transformed themselves into social, religious and spiritual relationships. It was considered so because it was irrevocable. Husband and wife could not dissolve it at will. They were bound to each other until death.

The concept that marriage was indissoluble, was a lofty one because it meant that the husband and wife after marriage have to adjust their tastes and tempers, their ideals and interests, instead of breaking with each other when they find that they differ. It thus involved sacrifices on the part of both husband and wife as each was called upon to overcome the incompatibility of the other. Hindu marriage, thus viewed, is not an ordinary affair wherein the weakness of flesh plays a dominant part. On the contrary, demands of personal gratification and pleasures are subordinated and the individual is called upon to make marriage a success by means of compromise and adjustment (Kapadia, 1958: 168-69). In other words, the sacramental nature of marriage sublimated sexual gratification into social, religious and spiritual aims.

According to Pandharinath Prabhu (1961) "Vivaha (marriage) is generally considered as obligatory for every person, because, in the first place, the birth of a son is said to enable one to obtain Moksha. Vivaha is one of the Sarir–Samskaras (sacraments sanctifying the body) through which every man and woman must pass. Manu considered it as a social institution for the regulation of proper relations between the sexes. With the evolution of Hindu marriage as a sacrament there has been an improvement in the status of woman compared to her status in the Vedic and Regvedic society. Tribal practices like bride price, selling and mortgaging of women, indiscriminate freedom for pre-marital and extra-marital relationships were forbidden. Chastity of women became the cardinal principle of marriage. The chastity of a woman reflected her character, pride and prestige of her family. A chaste woman came to be known as Pativrata. The term meant "one who is devoted to the husband" that is to say "one who follows her husband in what her husband bids her to do" (Sur, 1973: 68). A woman as wife, mother, sister etc was raised to the status of a goddess. In society a wife and mother commanded great respect and honour. However, this is not to suggest that women were accorded a higher status in society, especially in relation to men. The status of women continued to be low, so much so that her status suffered to a great extent in many respects in the family and society.

In their bid to protect the chastity of woman, men inflicted all kinds of tortures on women and exploited her to the maximum. As a daughter she never belonged to the parents' family, but considered only a guest biding her time until marriage. As a daughter-in-law she remained an outsider. A wife does not have any status as long as she does not bear children, especially sons. "Her greatest responsibility is to bear a child, preferably a son. Barrenness is a fear, a curse, an unending reproach" (Mandelbaum, 1970). The wife is solely held responsible if she does not bear children, but not the husband. A widow is not only not allowed to marry, but is also subjected to all kinds of ill-treatment and harassment, especially among the twice-born castes viz Brahmins, kshatriyas and vaishyas. Women were denied access to formal education and right to property. Women were equated with Shudras and were debarred from the study of theology and philosophy. Kautilya's Arthasastra prescribed punishment for immodest wives. Women, through the ages, have always been treated as the lesser sex (Ghosh, 1989: 10). A woman is expected to adjust to her parent-in-laws' household to which she goes after her marriage. She is placed under severe restrictions and has little or no say in decision-making and is directly subordinate to her mother-in-law. Her status the in family depends greatly on her husband's contribution to the family economy, and in middle and upper class families, on the amount of dowry brought by herself.

As Neera Desai (1957) puts it, ideologicaily woman was considered a completely inferior species, inferior to the male, having no significance, no personality; socially, she was kept in a state of subjection, denied any right, suppressed and oppressed. She was further branded as basically lacking the ethical fibre. The patriarchal joint family, the custom of polygamy, the purdha the property structure, early marriage, sati (self-immolation of the widows) or a state of permanent widowhood, all these contributed to the smothering of the free development of women. In short, women were given a very low status.

Changing Status of Women During the British

British rule in India may be said to have initiated significant changes in the status of woman. The British, compared to

Indians, were a liberal, secular, equalitarian and democratic people. Although the British came to India with the sole purpose of trade and commerce, in course of time, they began to establish their political rule in India. When they firmly entrenched themselves as political rulers, they launched social reforms to abolish age-old practices like Sati. Social reformers like Raja Rammohan Roy and William Bentick protested against evil customs like Sati and widowhood. It was the untiring efforts of Ishwar Chandra Vidyasagar that led to the promulgation of the Widow Remarriage Act of 1956, which made widow remarriage legal.

Another great landmark of the 19th century was the Civil Marriage Act of 1872, which was passed as a result of the bold initiative of Keshab Chandra Sen. Ishwar Chandra Vidyasagar believed that it was through education that women could developto her full stature.

Apart from social reformers, and political leaders, the British Govt. also contributed to bringing about changes in the attitudes of society towards women. With the establishment of a huge bureaucracy to run the administration of the country, schools and colleges, mills and factories, transport and communication facilities, modern education and white-collar occupations became available to women. British rule, thus, released the forces of modernisation. On the whole, the period after the 19th century, in respect of the status of women, was marked by: 1) attack on social evils, 2) social legislations, 3) female education, and 4) entry of women into modern occupations.

Status of Women After Independence

After Independence, India adopted democracy based on adult franchise. Political power came to be vested in every individual citizen to decide the future of the country. The traditional discriminations based on caste, religion and sex were abolished. Equality, secularism and social justice for the weak and oppressed became the cardinal principles of development.

The Preamble to the Constitution of India resolved to secure for all its citizens: Justice – Social, economic and political; Liberty of thought, expression, belief, faith and worship; Equality of Status and opportunity; and to promote among them a sense of Fraternity, assuring the dignity of the individual and the unity of the nation.

Under Article 38 of the Directive Principles of State Policy, the state shall strive to promote the welfare of the people by securing and protecting, as effectively as it may, a social order in which justice-social, economic and political-shall inform all the institutions of national life.

Article 16 (1) guarantees "equality of opportunity or appointment to any office under the State, and Article 16 (2) forbids discrimination in respect of any employment or office under the state on the ground only of place of birth, language residence or any one of them.

Article 39 assures women the right to equality in remuneration:

1. that the citizens, men and women equally, have the right to an adequate means of livelihood;
2. that there is equal pay for equal work for both men and women.

It is clear that the Constitution of India has provided for equal rights and privileges for men and women. Besides, the Govt. of India enacted a number of social legislations to raise the status of women. They are:

1. The Hindu Marriage Act, 1955,
2. The Hindu Succession Act, 1956,

3. Dowry Prohibition Act, 1961 etc.

Programmes to Raise the Status of Woman

In pursuance of the Constitutional guarantees provided for the development of women, a number of educational and economic programmes were planned. Besides health and welfare programmes, a number of educational and economic programmes were also undertaken. One of the major changes, which has occurred in Independent India is the importance given to the education of women. The planners have looked upon education as the chief agent of modernisation and social change. It was also believed that education was the crucial agent in achieving economic as well as political transformation. For modernizing India, education has been considered a significant determinant of aspiration, technology, productivity and mobility. Education, besides being given support as a means for women to fulfill their traditional domestic and familial roles, was considered a good lever for getting employment (Desai, 1988). Concerted efforts were made after independence to advance the education of girls and women. In the first decade after Independence, the enrolment of girls almost doubled. Special programmes included measures such as the appointment of school mothers, grants of scholarships and stipends, special prizes and free education to certain

TABLE III.1

Growth of Literacy Since Independence by Sex

Year	*Rate of Literacy Among Men*	*Rate of Literacy Among Women*	*Total Literacy Rate*
1951	24.95	07.93	16.67
1961	34.44	12.95	24.02
1971	39.52	18.70	29.48
1981	46.89	24.82	43.56
1991	63.86	37.42	52.11

Source: Mill Alam, "Literacy: The Key to Development", *Social Welfare*, Sept. '1992.

categories of girls. In secondary schools, provision was made for girls' hostels and proper transport facilities. Provision for separate high schools and colleges was made to encourage high school and college education among women.

Importance of Literacy for Women

Literacy, understood as the ability to read and write in ones language, is identified as an important instrument of social change. For example, elementary literacy enables women working in unorganised sectors both in rural and urban areas and also housewives to read signboards, prices mentioned on packets of consumer goods such as soap, salt, oil etc. Thus literacy helps women in getting their day-to-day transactions done with greater understanding and efficiency. A document of the Union Govt. rightly points out that literacy is the only pass-port for an illiterate or semi-literate for independent learning for gaining knowledge, bettering his/ her understanding and relying more and more upon his capacity to take his/her own decisions.

Data presented in Table III. 1 about the growth of literacy show that women are increasingly becoming literate since Independence. For example, the literacy rate for women rose from 07. 93 per cent in 1951 to 39. 12 percent in 1991. Indeed, it was a tremendous boost in the educational status of women. However, the rate of literacy for women, compared to that for men is far from satisfactory. Nevertheless, the fact that there is a definite improvement in the rate of female literacy shows that women are on the path of progress and development.

The enrolment of girls and women in schools and colleges, as indicated in Table III. 2 shows that girls enrolled themselves in greater numbers year after year. For example there were 36. 8 lakh girls in primary school in 1946-47, which rose to 244. 01 lakhs in 1973-74. Similarly there were 3. 2 lakh girls in middle schools in 1946-47, which rose to 45. 37 lakh in 1973-74. Data further showed that an increasing number of women enrolled in secondary schools, colleges and universities. On the basis of the available data, it can be stated that there has been a considerable rise in the educational status of women since independence.

TABLE III. 2

Education of Girls and Women

(in lakhs)

Years	*Primary School (Classes I-V)*	*Middle School (Classes VI-VII)*	*Secondary School (Classes VIII-XI)*	*Colleges and Universities (General Education)*
1	2	3	4	5
1946-47	36.8 (37)	3.2 (18)	0.7 (12)	0.16 (10)
1950-51	53.85 (39)	5.34 (20)	1.66 (15)	0.37 (14)
1955-56	76.39 (44)	8.67 (25)	3.29 (21)	0.75 (17)
1960-61	113.47 (48)	16.70 (32)	5.56 (23)	1.33 (22)
1965-69	182.93 (57)	28.46 (37)	12.05 (30)	2.91 (28)
1968-69	199.36 (59)	34.93 (39)	15.79 (32)	4.37 (30)
1973-74	244.01 (62)	45.37 (43)	23.40 (36)	9.0 (31)

Notes: 1. Figures in parentheses indicate the number of girls for every 100 boys enrolled.

2. Figures in the last column relate to enrolments at undergraduate, post graduate and research stages in general education arts, science and commerce courses.

Source: 1. Figures for school enrolment in 1950-51, 1960-61, 1965-66, and 1968-69 are from the Ministry of Education.

2. Figures for school enrolment in 1973-74 (target) are from the Draft Fifth Five Year Plan, 1974-79, Vol. II P. 197

3. Figure of enrolment in Colleges and universities are from Education in India for various years brought out by the Ministry of Education, New Delhi.

Employment of Women

A large majority of women from the backward and lower classes worked for wages in unorganised sectors like agriculture, construction etc. The employment was seasonal and unsecured at that. However, the advent of industrialization, modern education, and science and technology have revolutionized the occupational structure thereby paving the way for both men and women to be employed in large numbers on the basis of equal work, equal pay'. A large number of educated women are taking up white-collar jobs as goals of life. Women are increasingly becoming an integral part of the modern economic system.

The Planning Commission, until the Fourth Plan, identified three broad areas of development in the case of women, viz Education, Social Welfare and Health. In the Fifth Plan some attention was paid to generation of employment for women and the Sixth Plan for the first time devoted attention to the problem of unemployment among women.

Women in Labour Force

In the following pages an attempt is made to explain the status of women in the labour force.

According to the 1981 Census, of the total female main workers, a majority of them were engaged as cultivators and agricultural labourers (72%). Similarly, of the total female marginal workers a large majority (81%) of the women were working as cultivators and agricultural labourers. The proportion of women working as main and marginal workers in other services was also low. The data give a grim picture of the status of women in the labour force. But with the expansion of higher education a greater proportion of educated women have gained access to white-collar jobs.

Table III. 4 clearly shows that educated women are found in larger numbers in various professions in 1967, in the private

TABLE III. 3

Percentage-wise Distribution of Main Workers, Marginal Workers and Total Workers (Main Plus Marginal) by Industrial Categories, 1981

Industrial Category	*Main Workers*		*Marginal Workers*		*Total workers*		
	Male	*Female*	*Male*	*Female*	*Persons*	*Male*	*Female*
Total	100.00	100.00	100.00	100.00	100.00	100.00	100.00
I. Cultivators	47.70	32.20	41.66	47.91	42.06	43.66	37.50
II. Agricultural labourers	19.56	40.18	33.29	41.43	26.31	19.83	44.79
III. Livestock, forestry, Fishing, hunting and Plantations, orchards and allied activities	2.34	1.85	0.68	0.64	2.22	2.37	1.79
IV. Mining and quarrying	0.62	0.36	0.25	0.06	0.52	0.61	0.27
V. Manufacturing Processing, serving andd repairs							
(a) Household industry	3.1	4.5	3.0	4.0	3.5	3.1	4.4
(b) Other than household Industry	88.92	93.55	35.34	72.15	17.37	88.85	43.14
VI. Construction	1.81	0.80	1.95	0.39	1.52	1.81	0.66
VII. Trade and commerce	7.33	2.04	4.86	1.04	5.84	7.28	1.75
VIII. Transport, storage & Communications	3.32	0.38	1.71	0.06	2.51	3.29	0.29
IX. Others services	9.22	7.05	4.23	1.25	8.14	9.12	5.35

Note: According to the census of India (1981) work is defined as participation in any economically productive activity. Such participation may be physical or mental in nature. Work involves not only actual but also effective supervision and direction of work. The Census of India, 1981, has classified workers in two categories viz main workers who worked for part of the year preceding the date of enumeration and whose main activity was in either cultivation or as agricultural labourers or in household industry or in other works. However, marginal workers are those who have not worked for a major part of the preceding year concerned but nevertheless have done some work anytime during the preference period.

sector, and in 1968,in the public sector. Although there is heavy concentration of employed women in teaching, they are found in other sectors such as medical and health, telephone and clerical jobs too. The report of the committee on the status of women in India: Towards Equality (1974) has dealt with exhaustively in respect of the status of women in education and employment.

TABLE III. 4

Women in Selected Professions in Public and Private Sectors

(in lakhs)

Professionals	*Private sector (1967)*	*Public sector (1968)*
A. Teaching personnel		
1) Teachers- middle and primary Sc.	21,431	213,452
2) Teachers-secondary schools	32,686	28,260
3) Teachers-College & University	18,897	4,266
B. Medical and Health personnel		
1) Nurses	6,845	22,727
2) Midwives and health visitors	1,196	24,318
3) Nursing attendants and related workers	NA	23,818
4) Physicians and surgeons	NA	3,091
5) Ayahs and nurse maids	NA	5,675
C. Telephone Operators	5,052	1,051D.
Clerical and related workers		
1) Stenos	3,494	2,113
2) Ministerial assistants and clerks	6,226	67,623
3) Typists and teletypists	1,643	5,852

Source: Report of the Committee on Status of Woman in India, 1974: 205.

A large number of educated and semi-educated women are taking to self-employment under various self-employment schemes provided for women. A number of studies conducted on college students, women and working women (Kapur, 1970; Desai and Anantram, 1985; Ahmed, 1979; Ramanamma, 1979; Hate, 1969; Malika, 1960) have revealed that women, especially educated women, are becoming aware of their rights and privileges provided by the constitution of India. Although the incidence of crime-rape, dowry deaths etc - is on the increase, the present generation of women has relatively a modern view of life, compared to the traditional in their approach to life. To quote Dube (1963: 203): "The modern woman is gradually breaking through the shell of a narrow existence and rigid traditionalism. New horizons are opening up for woman in modern India. The changes are, no doubt, most apparent today at the level of the sophisticated urban elite, but gradually women of other sections are also being affected by this trend. The transition cannot naturally be rapid in a society that has been traditional-directed for several centuries. But the resistance of orthodoxy is gradually weakening".

4

Social Background of the Respondents

An analysis of the social background of the respondents forms an integral part of any sociological study. Such a discussion provides the study with a proper perspective and brings out the social complexion and the economic status of the respondents. There is a close relationship between social background and individuals personality. Social background acts as a motivating and restraining factors in the life of the respondents in times of crisis. It is the social background which prevents the individual from break-down. It influences one's efficiency in the work world. In a major study Uplaonkar (1988) has shown how one's social background influences the occupational aspirations of college students. An individual's social prestige is determined by his relative position on various parallel vertical prestige hierarchies like education, income etc. (Lengky, 1954; Landecker. 1963; Gold 1952).

The social background of the respondents plays a very important role in developing their sense or perception of responsibility. It influences their social self and world-view one's ability to adjust and manage in life depends to a great extent on one's social background. Besides a discussion about social background also helps in knowing whether the sample drawn for the study tends to be skewed or normally distributes.

In the present study the social background of the respondents is studies at two levels.

1. Personal and parental, and
2. Husband and parents-in-law.

1. Age Structure of the Respondents

TABLE IV.1

Respondents by Age

Age	*Frequency*	*Percentage*
Young	142	71
Adult	154	44
Old	54	15
	350	100

Age is an important factor in understanding the role and status of an individual in society (Persons, 1942, Benedier, 1938). Society differentiates human beings into children, adults and old on the basis of their age. Age composition of the respondents reveals whether the sample is young, adult or old, as responses of the respondents partly, are related to their age composition. Age composition of the respondents, as shown in Table IV. 1 shows that majority of the respondents were adults (44%) and young (41%) only 15 per cent of the respondents were old.

2. Religious Background of the Respondents

TABLE IV.2

Respondents by Religion

Religion	*Frequency*	*Percentage*
Hindu	236	67
Muslim	71	20
Christian	43	12
	350	100

Religion constitutes an important aspect of the Indian society. A look at Table IV.2 indicates that about 67 per cent of the respondents were Hindus. Muslims (20%) and Christians (12%) had a meagre representation in the study. The predominance of Hindus in the sample shows that Muslims and Christians were not finding access to modern occupations.

3. Educational Background

TABLE IV.3

Respondents by Education Level

Education Level	*Frequency*	*Percentage*
Graduation	184	53
Post Graduation	166	47
	350	100

Education, as imparted in schools and colleges, has come to be accepted as an agent of social change and modernisation. It develops the skills of reading, writing and numeracy. It also develops the capacity of reasoning, thinking and comprehension. It introduces dynamic elements in one's personality. Education, in the form of degrees, is intimately linked with modern occupations. The educated find better employment opportunities.

An analysis of the data in Table IV.3 shows that the proportion of the graduates (53%) is more than that of the post-graduates (47%). It can be said that the respondents came from the middle and upper classes.

4. Rural-Urban Background

The rural-urban background plays a significant role in determining one's life chances and life styles. Whether one spends one's early childhood and teen age in a village or city makes all the difference for one's employment opportunities and social mobility in life. Generally urban people have a greater share in modern education and occupations. Our sample also shows that a majority of the respondents were drawn from the urban background. For example, 70% of the urban women, as against 30% of the rural figures in the sample. It means a great majority of the working women were drawn from the towns and cities.

TABLE IV.4

Respondents by Rural Urban Background

Place	*Frequency*	*Percentage*
Rural	108	30
Urban	242	70
	350	100

5. Marital Status

TABLE IV.5

Respondents by Marital Status

Marital Status	*Frequency*	*Percentage*
Married	250	72
Unmarried	100	28
	350	100

Marriage is an important event in the life of an individual. This is more so in the case of women. It redefines one's role and status in society. In India married women are respected and honoured. Marital status indicates whether or not one is settled in life. It shows one's desire for family and kinship. It provides for a bigger and a broader vision of life. It also indicates a will power to know and face life. It enable a broader would view.

Data collected with regards to marital status shows that out of 350 respondents 250 or 75 per cent were married. Twenty five per cent were not married. Marital status of the respondents shows that the sample drawn is conformity with the objective of studying the problems and prospects of working women.

6. Occupational Status of the Respondents

TABLE IV.6

Respondents by Occupational Status

Occupational Level	*Frequency*	*Percentage*
High	145	30
Middle	100	28
Low	105	42
	350	100

Occupation in terms of gainful employment is a crucial factor in deciding one's position and status in society. A study of occupational status of the respondents explains their power, position and income. Data presented in Table 6 about the occupational status of the respondents show that 42 per cent were working in low level jobs such as clerks, school teachers etc., similarly, 28 per cent were engaged in middle level jobs like administrators, supervisors, college teachers. Respondents pursuing occupations like doctors, principals, managers etc., accounted for 30 per cent. Data reveal that the respondents represented all levels of occupations.

7. Salary of the Respondents

TABLE IV.7

Salary Per Annum of the Respondents

Salary	*Frequency*	*Percentage*
High	119	34
Medium	147	42
Low	84	24
	350	100

The salary one draws in intimately associated with one's standard of living. Information regarding the salary of the respondents shows that 42 per cent were drawing a medium salary between Rs. 50,0000 and Rs. 75,000 per year while 34 per cent were drawing a high salary i. e. above Rs. 75,000 per year while 34 per cent were drawing a high salary i. e. above Rs. 75,000 per annum. Respondents drawing a low salary, say below Rs. 50,000 per year, constituted 24 percentage. Data, as shown in Table 7, show that the respondents, under the study belonged to the middle class.

8. Length of Service of the Respondents

TABLE IV.8

Length of Service of the Respondents

Length of Service	*Frequency*	*Percentage*
Below 3 years	50	15
3 years to 8 years	147	42
9 years to 14 years	117	33
15 years and above	36	10
	350	100

Length of service in a job reveals incumbent's amount of experience, salary, promotion etc. Employees with short length of service settled and exposed to the world. It can be seen the while 42 per cent of the respondents had 3 to 8 years of

9. Family Background

TABLE IV.9

Respondents According to Family Background

Item	*Frequency*	*Percentage*
Joint Family	200	57
Nuclear Family	150	43
	350	100

service, 33 per cent had 9 to 14 years of service. The remaining to per cent had more than 15 per cent had more than 15 years of service. Only 15 per cent were new comers with less than 3 years of service. By and large a majority of the respondents and enough service.

Data were collected from the respondents about whether they were staying in joint or nuclear families. The respondents were asked to give the number of members living together in the family and their relationship with each other. The meaning of joint family and nuclear family was broadly understood. The respondents who stayed with their husbands and children along with their married and unmarried brothers and unmarried sisters, parents-in-law were said to live in joint family. The respondents who lived with their husbands and children in a separate household were treated as nuclear family. However, it was observed that there were no cent per cent joint or nuclear families. There were nuclear families where the respondents had to live with a temporary parent-in-law or brother/sister-in-law for one or the reason. From Table 9 it can be seen that 57 per cent of the respondents were living in joint families, while 43 per cent in nuclear. The data clearly show that still a majority of the working women, under investigation, lived in joint families. However, the fact that 43 per cent of the respondents lived in nuclear families showed that a substantial proportion of working women preferred to establish separate households.

Respondents Parents' Background

Parents educational and occupational status has a deep impact on the development of their children's personality. Parents education and occupation act as source of motivation for educational and occupational choices. Thus the parents educational and occupational status will give a boost to the childrens progress and mobility.

Fathers' Education

TABLE IV.10

Fathers' Education

Educational level	*Frequency*	*Percentage*
Low	100	28
Middle	111	32
High	139	40
	350	100

Among all kin-members, the father is an important person in the family. He not jointly manages and supervises family but also acts as an agent of socialisation and role models. Therefore, his educational and occupational background has a deep bearing on the children's educational and occupational achievements. Data presented in Table IV.10 regarding Fathers education background showed that 28 per cent of them low education, that is they were illiterates or had studied up to primary level. Of the remaining 32 per cent had medium level education between SSLC and graduations and 40 per cent had higher education post graduate, professionals. A majority of the fathers had a good educational background.

Fathers' Occupation

TABLE IV.11

Fathers' Occupation

Occupation	*Frequency*	*Percentage*
Low	70	20
Medium	78	22
High	202	58
	350	100

Low=Agriculture, Medium= Business, High=Government Servant

Like his educational status the father's occupation is

equally important in influencing children's occupational aspirations. Children of employed fathers tend to be employed in life. Employed fathers tend to provide a congenial and favourable atmosphere for their children to as fire to go in for white-collar jobs. Thus the fathers' occupation has a influence on their children.

It can be seen from Table IV.9 that a majority (58%) of the fathers were draw for white-collar jobs, while 21 per cent of them were engaged in business. Only 20 per cent of them were engaged in agriculture. It could be stated that the respondents, under the study had a very complacent status as regards fathers' occupation.

Mothers' Education

TABLE IV.12

Mother's Education

Mother's Education	*Frequency*	*Percentage*
Low	208	60
Middle	86	25
High	56	15
	350	100

Like the fathers' education, the mothers' education is equally important for the development of the children's personality. Children have a more intimate and fact-to-face relationship with their mothers than fathers. Mothers education is especially important for the daughters than the boys, for it is the mother more than the father, who acts as role model for her daughters.

Indian women in the past were backward to receive formal education. Mothers in the past could not play any role in developing their daughters career with independence, women's education has become a part of national policy.

Today educated women are playing an important role in the advancement of the family and society. Data on mothers' education indicate that 25 and 15 per cent of mother had studied upto the middle and higher levels, respectively. But 60 per cent had education (illiterates or upto middle schools). Although the mothers education seems to be poor it should be viewed against the historical background of women's status in India.

Mothers' Occupation

TABLE IV.13

Mother's Occupation

Mother's Occupation	*Frequency*	*Percentage*
Low (House Wife)	276	78
High (Govt. Servant)	74	22
	350	100

Like the fathers' occupation, the mothers' occupation plays an important role in influencing the growth of personality of the children. This is more in the case of daughters as there is a close interaction between the mothers and daughters. A working mother who is more higher educated has had a larger explosive in enlightened can better develop modern values and ambition for top-notch employment among the daughters than a non-working women.

Data presented in Table IV.13 shows that 78 per cent of the mothers were housewives while 22 per cent were employed. It shows the proportion of working mothers of the respondents was small.

Summing Up

The respondents' personal background revealed that they were young and adults, and were Hindus. Respondents who were highly educated came from an urban background. A majority of them married and were employed in middle level and higher level jobs. A majority were found to draw a hand some salary and had put in a pretty long length of service in their jobs. The respondents fathers had a good educational background and a majority were in white-collar jobs. But most mothers had have poor education and only small proportion of them were employed.

HUSBANDS AND PARENTS-IN-LAW'S SOCIAL BACKGROUND

Husbands' Education

TABLE IV.14

Husbands' Education

Husbands Education	*Frequency*	*Percentage*
Low	14	6
Middle	40	16
High	196	78
	250	100

Low=SSLC, Middle=Graduates, High=Post Graduates

There is a close relationship between the educational status of the working wives and their husbands' educational status. Educated working wives have generally tended to select husbands with higher educational and occupational status than they them selves have. It can be seen from the table 14 that an overwhelming majority (83%) of the husbands had college and university education. Only 13 and 4 per cents had studied upto higher secondary and primary level, respectively. It means the respondents husbands were highly educated.

It is to be generally observed that employed women tend to select employed husbands. Similarity in the occupational status of husbands and wives is supposed to yield better cooperation and understanding between the spouses.

Husbands' Occupation

TABLE IV.15

Husbands' Occupation

Husbands Occupation	*Frequency*	*Percentage*
Low	54	22
High	196	78
	250	100

Low=business, High=White-collar

It can be seen from the data on the husbands occupations that an overwhelming majority (78%) of the husbands were engaged a white collar jobs, while 22 per cent were engaged in business. There appears to be some relationship between the occupations of the couple.

Parents-In-Law's Background

Parent-in-laws socioeconomic background is significantly related to the role and status of the daughters-in-law, especially when they are employed. For employed educated and employed parents-in-law are likely to understand family problems from a positive view point, such parents-in-law tend to resolve issues through mutual exchange of views and dialogues.

Father-in-law's Education

TABLE IV.16

Father-in-laws Education

Education	*Frequency*	*Percentage*
Low	125	50
Middle	75	30
High	50	20
	250	100

Father-in-laws as heads of families, will play a significant part in supervising administering and managing the family. Their educational status has a significant bearing on the progress and welfare of the family. Information gathered about father-in-laws education shows that 50 per cent had studied upto primary schools. But 30 per cent of the father-in-laws had studied upto the 7th standards, while a 20 per cent segment included PUC pass and undergraduates. The educational status of the fathers-in-laws was not very high.

Father-in-laws Occupation

TABLE IV.17

Father-in-laws Occupation

Occupation	*Frequency*	*Percentage*
Low	55	22
Middle	115	46
High	80	32
	250	100

Low=Agriculture, Middle=Business, High=Govt. Servant

The occupational status of the father-in-laws an important factor which influences interrelations of different members of the family. Father-in-laws working in white-collar jobs with their better communications skills can take recourse to democratic means to resolve stresses and strains in the family.

As the occupational background of the fathers-in-law shows table. 17 46 per cent of them were engaged in business. While 32 per cent of them were engaged in white-collar jobs; 22 per cent were pursuing agriculture. By and large the education background of the fathers-in-laws seemed to be relatively favourable.

Mother-in-laws Education

TABLE IV.18

Mother-in-laws Education

Education	*Frequency*	*Percentage*
Low	145	58
Middle	75	30
High	30	12
	250	100

The socio-economic status of the mother-in-law has a deep and lasting effect on the smooth working of the family. An educated mother-in-law can have a special insight into the problems of daughter-in-law so as to be able to find out suitable solution. Such mothers-in-laws can be less authoritarian in dealing with family problems.

A majority of the mothers-in-laws were illiterates. About 30 per cent of the education only upto the 7th standard. Only 12 per cent had completed SSLC. It can be said that educationally the mother-in-law were relatively backward.

Mother-in-laws Occupation

TABLE IV.19

Mother-in-laws Occupation

Occupation	*Frequency*	*Percentage*
Low	175	70
High	75	30
	250	100

Low=Housewife, High= Employed

By and large women in India have been engaged in house hold duties. Their entry into business and modern occupations is a recent phenomenon whether a mother-in-law is working or non-working makes all the difference for the peace and happiness of the family. For example a working mother-in-law can better understand the problems of a working daughter-in-law. A working mother-in-law also means more income, more facilities etc. It can be seen from Table 18 that an overwhelming majority (70%) were housewives. About 30 per cent were working as peons, clerks, school teachers etc. On the whole the parent-in-laws had an ordinary educational occupational background.

To sum up, a majority of husbands of the respondents were highly educated and engaged in white-collar jobs. The educational and occupational profile of the respondents parents-in-laws were not very flattering (or you can say 'high').

5

Modernisation of Working Women

The role and status of the employed woman depend upon the extent she has become modern in her attitudes, values and outlooks temper in her value orientations towards social issues as mentioned above towards social issues viz. woman's education and employment, marriage and family. To be specific, to what extent the employed woman has adopted modern values such as liberalism, rationalism, egalitarianism and scientific.

The present chapter is devoted to knowing to what extent employment, of course, and education, too, has brought about changes in the attitudes of working women towards woman's education and employment and marriage and family. Studies conducted by Sethi (1993), Ramanamma (1979), Mishra (1993), Lalitha Devi (1982), Agrawal (1986) and Sharma (1990) have found significant changes in the attitudes of educated and employed women. The studies, nevertheless, are not clear as to how tradition and modernity are reflected in their attitudes. In the following pages it is intended to analyse the attitudes of the employed woman towards woman's education and employment.

EMPLOYED WOMAN AND WOMAN'S EDUCATION

Education in modern India has become the most influential instrument of modernisation (Dube, 1974). Even prior to

Independence, education had led to the mobilization of peoples' aspiration for nationalization, liberalism and freedom. Educated Indians, even though few in number, were mainly responsible for carrying forward not only a movement for independence but also a relentless struggle for social and cultural reforms. Education, as an agent of socialisation, plays a great role in transforming an individual's personality. For example, education in terms of literacy provides the ability to read and write and enables the person to acquire the skills of elementary mathematics. Literacy is an indication of exposure to modern views and ideas and is, therefore, crucial for an overall analysis, especially that of women's status.

According to Inkeles (1969) modern education helps women in moving away from traditionalism to modernity. Anderson and Shills (1966) said that rapid change in social values and existing norms of a developing country can take place only when there is spread of female education.

Education at higher levels will develop one's rational faculty, thinking and reasoning power. Higher education empowers men and women to examine the causes and effects of events in life. Higher education in terms of certificates and degrees is intimately linked with white-collar jobs. Besides, education enhances one's self-image and develops independence and autonomy and thus provides aspiration for social mobility.

It is widely believed that women's education leads to:

1. Greater participation of females in the labour market.
2. Reduction in family size.
3. Greater attention by mothers to the care of their children in terms of health, character building and educational at accomplishment, and,

4. Greater per capita capital and income and better quality of human capital as a result of (2) and (3) above.

1. Women's Education in India

By and large formal education in terms of reading, writing, and mathematics was not thought necessary for women in ancient times. Since women were supposed to be ritually impure they were enjoined not to receive any education which was mostly associated with sacred scriptures and religious texts. William Adam (1868), who made enquiries in Bengal on the problem of education in his second report in the year 1835 AD, observed that it was common superstition that women who were taught to read and write became widows soon after their marriage; secondly, people believed that intrigues were facilitated by imparting literacy to women.

With the advent of the British there was considerable change in the attitude of society towards women's education. Schools and colleges were increasingly made available to women. Women's education received further impetus with the Indian govt's commitment to provide equality of opportunity to all after Independence. Separate schools and colleges were being established for women.

According to Cormack (1953:52) women's education was given further impetus by the growing desire of educated men to marry educated brides. According to Joshi (1973), besides other factors, the following were the factors for the improvement in female education at the University level:

(a) Because the age of girls marriage has increased, in such a situation she likes to continue education.

(b) Because educated boys want to marry an educated girl,

(c) For becoming self-supporting in life, and

(d) For status assurance and economic independence.

Girls were increasingly encouraged to seek more education; changing values gave further impetus to women's education. A highly educated girl, is now more acceptable as a bride than one without (or less) education because of here potential for employment and because an educated woman is an advantage in social mobility. The break up of the JF and emergence of the NF and increasing urbanisation are other factors encouraging the education of women.

(a) Attitude Towards Aims of Higher Education in Relation to Women

Although education has come to stay as an instrument of modernization in any society, its aims and objectives vary from caste to caste, class, religion and sex. In the present context of women's education there are differences of opinion. One line of thinking is that women should be given education to play their traditional roles as wife and mother. According to Promilla Kapur (1970) the traditional view of women's education was not to make women into efficient and active units in the process of socioeconomic and political development but to make them more capable of fulfilling their traditional role in society as wives and mothers. In other words, education for women was regarded as a means to improve their status within the family, and not to equip them to play any role in the wider social context (148-149). While the other way of approach is to train them for the challenges of modern life. Still others view that women must be given higher education to seek employment. It was intended in this part of the thesis to know how employed women perceived the aim of higher education with regard to women in modern India.

Opinions of the respondents to the above points were collected after a detailed discussion. The data presented in Table V. I show that 70 per cent of the respondents believed that the chief aim of women's education was to make them play their traditional roles as wives and mothers as well as equip them for taking active part in public life. The fact that emerged was that only 20 per cent believed that the aim of women's education was to prepare women for traditional roles. Only 10 per cent perceived the aim of women's education as seeking employment. A further discussion revealed that the working women under study had a broader perspective of education.

TABLE V.1

In Your Opinion What are the Aims of Higher Education with Regard to Women?

Aims	*Frequency*	*Percentage*
Makes them play woman's traditional role of wife better	70	20
Makes them fit for modern life	245	70
Enables them to seek employment	35	10
	350	100

(a) Level of Education for Women

There is an increasing realisation of the fact that education in principle has become imperative for all irrespective of caste, class, religion and sex. But at the same time it should be borne in mind that education itself is influenced by forces of caste, class, religion, and sex. Education is functionally related to social conditions. For example, rural people expect education to make women fit in with rural society.

TABLE V.2

Distribution of Respondent's Opinion: In Your Opinion How Much Education Should Women be Given? Specify Reasons

Level of Education	*Frequency*	*Percentage*
College/	175	50
PGSSLC	140	40
Middle School	25	10
	350	100

The Table V.2 shows that working women, under the study, have indicated a positive attitude towards women's education. For example, 50 per cent of the respondents wanted women to receive at least graduation/post graduation. Those who favoured graduation for women said that higher education not only helped them in securing employment, and of course a life-partner, but also developed the ability to participate in public life.

However, those who favoured only SSLC as the maximum education for women stressed that since the majority of the women reside in villages and towns, where the level of literacy is very low, higher education for women creates problems for marital prospects. There are many instances of graduate and post graduate women remaining unmarried for not securing more educated men, suited to their own level of education. One respondent said: " A graduate boy can accept a matriculate girl in marriage but a graduate girl would not accept a matriculate boy in marriage". Some also said that highly educated women develop a sense of ego and begin to look down upon less educated members in the family. Another respondent said: "Highly educated women develop a sense of aversion for domestic drudgery such as cleaning utensils, washing clothes, etc. More education endangers their role and status". Interestingly, 10 per cent of interviewees believed that women must be given education up to middle school. They argued that since the majority of the women in rural areas are supposed to look after their family, middle school (up to 7th) is enough for them. One respondent said "More education spoils women's character and makes them unfit to shoulder family responsibilities". In conclusion it may be said that the respondents felt that there was a relationship between level of education and women's role and status. The majority of our sample believed in medium level of education for common women. The findings of Kumud Ranjan (1993),

Pratima Kumari (1988), Sethi (1976), have indicated favourable response towards higher education.

Education and Traditional Role

This section deals with the influence or effect of education in developing efficiency of traditional roles of women such as wife' mother and as social being. The aim is to know how the sample perceived the modernising impact of education on the traditional roles of women as wife, mother and social women. The role of a wife has to be defined in relation to her husband's personal needs such as food, shelter, clothing, and sex, wife as manager and head.

A better wife in this study is conceptualised as the one who is aware of her responsibilities, duties and obligations as wife, who has a positive attitude towards the problems of her husband and who (wife) is a friend, philosopher and guide.

1. Working Woman as a Better Wife

TABLE V.3

Do You Think the Educated Wife will Become a Better Wife?

Response	*Frequency*	*Percentage*
Yes	280	80
No	70	20
	350	100

Inderjeet Kaur (1983) in her thesis "Status of Hindu Women in India" points out that modern education has had a deep impact on women's outlook; the values which they cherished under the influence of tradition are undergoing a radical transformation. In fact a new concept of womanhood is emerging in India which is at odds with the traditional concept of woman as devout wife confined to hearth and home. The Indian woman is not only the manager of the household but an active participant in public life today (p. 5). Studies by Altekar (1962), Shashi Jain (1988) show that under the impact of modern education and employment a process of role differentiation both in the family and public life has set in. The educated woman is playing her traditional roles as wife and mother much better. Shashi Jain (1988) points out: " Modern housewife is now called to perform many functions in her family which were hitherto exclusively in the domain of male members only. Recent changes have brought about not only the diversification of roles to be performed by the housewife but they have also brought about a new pattern of role-differentiation in terms of household functions to be performed by the wives and husbands". In Jain's opinion the higher educational achievements of the women and the economic influence of their family are the most important reasons responsible for opening new horizons of housewife's role both inside and outside her family.

In traditional setup, a woman, whether single or married, played a very conventional role in household matters. The relationships between husband and wife were, and are even today, characterised by one of superiority and inferiority. The husband was invested with all power and was responsible for administrative matters of the family. However, the hierarchical relations between husband and wife are transforming into egalitarian ones. To a question whether or not educated woman would become a better wife, an overwhelming majority (80%) gave a positive reply. A discussion with them revealed that educated wife could better look after social and personal needs such as food, shelter, clothing, health etc. of the family. It was also observed that an educated wife could act as a manager of the household. The respondents said an educated wife is capable of looking after family problems and issues from a broader perspective in the interest of all and resolved them with mutual consultation and discussion. The responses of the working wives, under study, also revealed that they believed in establishing more harmonious interpersonal relations with their husbands and other members of the family. To conclude, the working women, under the study, believed that education helped them in playing their traditional role as wives from a modern, scientific and rational points of view.

Working Woman as a Better Mother

The educated employed woman in modern society is emerging with better abilities and capacities to face the challenges of traditional roles. Under the impact of modernization the traditional roles of woman are becoming specialised. She is applying scientific knowledge to her roles. The higher education of women and their entry into employment has brought a radical change in the concept of child rearing and these factors are remarkably influencing the "Socialising role of woman as a mother " (Chakrapani & V. Kumar , 1994).

The chief functions of a woman as mother are bearing and rearing. In traditional society bearing and rearing of children were conducted according to customary practices. But these practices, more often than not, were not based on any scientific knowledge. According to Shashi Jain (1988) further "In practical and daily life, her function of motherhood was simply keeping the child fed and clothed. She was not responsible for the socialization of her children. A mother had a limited role in her children's upbringing, education and marriages settlements. To be precise, she had no voice in the family and social matters. With the growth of modern education revolutionary changes have been introduced in the philosophy and practice of bearing and rearing of children. Shashi Jain (1988) points out that in modern times, the educated mother's role has become differentiated as the demands of the new situations involve the inculcation of new values among children. Educated women have become conscious of the importance of pregnancy and upbringing of children.

TABLE V.4

Do You Think an Educated Woman can Become a Better Mother?

Response	*Frequency*	*Percentage*
Yes	280	80
No	70	20
	350	100

The respondents were asked to report whether or not an educated woman would become a better mother. Almost 80 per cent of them gave a positive reply. They said that the educated woman would take all necessary steps and precautions about pregnancy and adopt scientific measures to bear and rear children. For example, during pregnancy they would go to a doctor for regular check up and follow the course of treatment prescribed by the doctor. A similar method would be adopted to rear the children. To conclude, the employed woman felt that education has helped to equip her as an efficient mother.

The Working Woman and Management of Home

The aim of this section was to analyse whether or not an educated woman could become a good or efficient manager of her home. The term "Manage" was understood as efficient planning, organising, controlling income and expenditure, household chores and looking after relatives, guests and friends.

Education has far reaching effects on the development of personality. Education of woman helps in developing a new consciousness and desire for improvement. The traditional woman learnt the skills of management through experience. Because of illiteracy, ignorance and lack of exposure to the external world, she could not apply her mind. But educated woman is likely to pay attention to standard of living and children's education.

TABLE V.5

Do You Think the Educated Woman can Become a Good Manager of Her Home?

Response	*Frequency*	*Percentage*
Yes	315	85
No	35	15
	350	100

The data presented in Table V.5 show that an overwhelming majority (85%) replied that educated woman could manage her home much better compared to her counterpart in traditional society. While substantiating their statement they said that they made a monthly budget and tried to save money by avoiding unnecessary expenses. They believed in saving time, money and energy and utilitise the same for investing in useful activities. The respondents further pointed out that educated woman attended relatives, guests and friends better by under standing their needs. To quote Ramanamma and Bambawale (1982) "Educated woman can manage her own shopping, banking and take decisions at rudimentary levels. Her new role is that of a companion to her husband. She is considered responsible enough to advise, guide or discuss important issues with the husband. She is an independent entity in her own right". To conclude, educated woman can manage her home in response to the challenges of modern life.

Working Woman and Social Nature

A final point we wanted to know was whether or not educated woman is sociable in her nature. Boys and girls who attend schools and colleges are provided with opportunities to interact with each other. The word 'sociable' is a relative term. It refers to free mixing with people without caste, class, religious and sex inhibitions. It is understood as empathy, the ability to take on another's role and thus become aware of his / her feelings, as well as his / her motives, attitudes, values and belief. It is also understood as working with people and groups with open-mindedness and establishing a positive interpersonal relation. Education imparted in schools and colleges involves a greater degree of scientific temper, which enables individuals to discard attitudes, values and practice based on blind beliefs and superstitions. Educated women relatively tend to interact with men and women with a greater degree of sociability.

TABLE V.6

Do You Think an Educated Woman Will be Social?

Response	*Frequency*	*Percentage*
Yes	280	80
No	70	20
	350	100

The respondents were asked; do you think educated woman is more sociable? It should be noted that 76 per cent of the respondents indicated that the educated woman could become a sociable person. During the discussion it was stressed that an educated woman was open to free interaction with people without inhibitions and had a sense of empathy about the needs and problems of others. Some members also believed in earning goodwill of others through positive communications.

Summary

In this section an attempt was made to know the views of the working women, under the study, about woman's education and its significance in relation to woman's role and status. The analysis revealed that the respondents had a favourable attitude towards woman's education. They said that modern education must equip women for both traditional and modern roles and statuses. The respondents held that modern education helped them to play their traditional roles, such as wife and mother, more efficiently. They also believed that education developed in them more sociability. To conclude, modern education has a positive effect on the attitudes and values of women in India.

Working Women and Attitude Towards Employment of Woman

The emerging status of working woman depends upon the role she plays in modern society, and the role, in turn, hinges upon her attitude towards employment as a career. If employment is chosen as a temporary measure or for sheer economic need, in that case such employed women cannot play any positive, constructive and meaningful role in modern society. The following questions are raised in this regard.

1. Why do women take to employment?
2. Who motivates for employment?
3. Should women continue to work after they are married?

The working woman is comparatively a new phenomenon in modern India. Employment outside the home represents a major role innovation for married women (Kanna and Vargese, 1978: 89). The growth, expansion and diversification of modern education and occupations with the provision for equality of opportunity in educational, occupational and political spheres, there has been a spurt in the employment of educated women, especially in organized sector. Besides, changing concepts of standard of living in urban areas and work-values have promoted educated women to seek employment opportunity.

Employment of women has come to stay as an integral part of the economic organization in modern India.

Motivation For Employment

1. Reasons for Taking Up Employment

The reasons that compel women to take us employment have far-reaching implications for their emerging status in modern India. It is generally believed that women, especially married, take to gainful employment out of sheer economic necessity to supplement family income. Although it was true a few decades ago, this does not hold good today. Although economic factors are responsible for educated women taking to employment, there are a few other factors such as social, socio-psychological, legal and demographic, which have contributed towards the changing status of women in contemporary society. Today women take up jobs in order to use their talents, achieve a status of their own, be economically independent, get freedom to mix with others, overcome the boredom of remaining at home and finally to satisfy their ambition of having a career. Gainful employment is believed by women to be the means of acquiring equality of status. According to the Labour Bureau's Report, four basic factors, which have been responsible for woman's employment, particularly the employment of mother, are:

1. Permanent and growing inadequacy of the income of the principal breadwinner.
2. Temporary fall in the family's income due to exceptional or accidental circumstances such as the sickness and premature incapacitation of the principal earning member.
3. The death of the bread winner, and
4. A woman's desire for economic independence or for securing a higher standard of living for the family.

Several factors have contributed for women's employment in modern India.

(a) The increasing proportion of educated women has created a pool of eligible workers.

(b) A growing awareness of the emerging fact that a single person's income is inadequate to maintain a decent standard of living.

(c) There is a shift in the attitude towards women's employment.

A number of studies have tried to investigate into the reasons why women take to employment (Jain, 1998; Mathur, 1992; Ranjan, 1993). But it is not clear whether or not women are taking to employment as a temporary measure or career. Manjula (1990) conducted a study of unmarried working women. The study revealed that unmarried working women were of the view that they were firm to in their job even after marriage. They said they would not sacrifice employment for marriage. C. Rajgopalan in his article "Role-perception and Role-performance" tested the hypothesis that individuals who make a careful and intelligent choice of achievement roles are less likely to repent their choice subsequently and hence may not be driven to change their roles on that ground.

TABLE V.7

What are the Main Reasons for Taking Up a Job?

Item	*Frequency*	*Percentage*
Want to support myself	175	50
Raise the standard of the family	88	26
Secure economic independence	87	24
	350	100

The respondents were asked the following question; What are the main reasons for taking up a job?

It could be seen from the data presented in Table V.7 that 50 per cent of the respondents said they wanted to support themselves, while 26 per cent were interested in raising the living standard of the family. Similarly, the remaining 24 per cent were for securing economic independence. A further probe into their statements revealed that a majority of the respondents wanted to be economically self-dependent, not be dependent on others, including parents or husbands. An office supervisor said: "In modern times with the increase in the age of marriage and the growing, incidence of dowry, educated women cannot afford to depend on their parents for long. Hence, employment has become a dire necessity". Another high school teacher said: "Employment acts as a security in case of contingencies like husband's death or accident". According to Ralph H. Turner (1974) women seek intrinsic rewards through their education and occupation. Their station in life and the corresponding level of living is determined by their husbands' occupation but their life is empty unless they are themselves engaged in some work. It follows that the reason for women's employment is beyond economic need. Our findings agree with the findings of Vanita Srivastava (1978). On analysing the data gathered by Srivastav, it is indicated that comparatively a much lower proportion of working women felt that they were working for economic reasons. Srivastava's data show that 38 per cent of working women said that the economic factor was the most important reason, 22 per cent said that they worked in order to improve the family's standard of living and as many as 40 per cent said that they worked mainly for non-economic reasons (p. 143).

To quote Kapur (1978) "Educated women are gradually realising that work is not a necessary evil, but a way of living a full life and provides a possibility for self realisation " (p. 119).

To sum up, working women, under study, believed that employment enabled them to establish themselves as individuals with their economic security guaranteed. It was also found that employment helped them in maintaining a high standard of living, and thus conferred a high social status on the incumbent.

Sources of Motivation for Employment

Motivation is a complex phenomenon. It is not possible, it is even wrong to pinpoint exactly one factor as the source of motivation. Always it is a group of factors that play an important role in providing motivation. Although different theories of human motivation are proposed (Maslow, 1954; Herzberg, 1959; Maclelland, 1961), no theory explains the complex process of motivation in full. There may be two sources of motivation:

1) External, and 2) Internal. Motivation may be acquired from without viz parents, kith and kin, husband, peers etc. Motivation may be from within: self. In practical life there cannot be a watertight compartment between the two sources of motivation. Both operate together in varying degrees. Our objective is to know whether the respondents were influenced and inspired by external factors or inner ones or both. To be specific, we would like to know who played a major role in motivating the respondents to seek employment.

In the case of 50 per cent of the respondents (see Table V.8) it was the parents/husband/kith and kin who acted as the main source of motivation. It means the parents/husbands/kith and kin themselves are interested and are involved in helping their women-folk. But, interestingly, 40 per cent of the respondents were self-motivated. That is, they themselves were looking for a job. A small proportion (10%) of the respondents were influenced by friends and neighbours.

TABLE V.8

Who Motivated You to Take Up the Present Job?

Item	*Frequency*	*Percentage*
Parents/husband/kith&kin	175	50
Self	140	40
Friends and neighbours	35	10
	350	100

From the data it was clear that parents, husbands and kith and kin had provided the motivation for taking to employment, but a substantial proportion of the respondents (40%) were themselves becoming employment or career oriented. It shows educated women were coming forward on their own in search of jobs and occupations. In the discussion that followed it was found that although motivation for employment came from external forces, the respondents themselves had a strong desire for employment. The parents and husbands provided the necessary social sanctions to the motivation of the respondents. The proposition may be hazarded that respondents with self-motivation for employment are likely to play the role of agents of social change and modernisation.

Attitude Towards Continuing in Job After Marriage

It is generally believed that educated women will have taken to employment, in the first distance, as a temporary measure till they would get married, that they would have their jobs in mid-career to devote themselves wholly to domestic responsibilities. Recent trends in women's participation in gainful work have shown that employment of women is becoming an established phenomenon. Diversification of occupations, better employment opportunities for educated, job security, attractive scales and remuneration, introduction of pension provision even in the private sector have facilitated women's taking to employment as a full-time job or career. Marriage is not believed to come in the way of employment. On the contrary, more employed than non-employed women are preferred in marriage.

TABLE V.9

Do You Think Employed Women should Continue in Their Job After Marriage?

Response	*Frequency*	*Percentage*
Yes	315	88
No	35	12
	350	100

It can be seen that the overwhelming majority (88%) of the respondents were in favour of employed women continuing in their job even after marriage. It was only in the case of 12 % that opinion was in favour of the working woman giving up her job and devoting herself to her family after marriage. While substantiating their reply a majority of those who gave a positive reply said that career and marriage were not incompatible with each other. On the contrary, they said career was becoming an integral part of the family goals in modern society. The respondents said that they could manage both career and married life and there was no need to sacrifice career for marriage. In fact, they argued, with employment married life becomes relatively rich. The small 12 per cent who did not agree with the statement said that married working women could not do justice to both career and family. According to them, employment exerted strains on married life. To conclude, a majority of the working women believed that one need not give up her job after marriage.

Attitude Towards Employment Versus Marriage

Another attempt was made to know the attitudes of working women towards employment vis-à-vis marriage.

TABLE V.10

If a Working Woman is to Make a Choice Between Career and Getting Married, What Should She Choose?

Item	*Frequency*	*Percentage*
Job	70	20
Marriage	37	12
Both	243	68
	350	100

At times a conflict arises between job and marriage. Reactions of the respondents as shown in Table V.10 reveal that job and marriage could not be put against each other in terms of "this or that". Only 20 per cent of them preferred career at the cost of marriage, while 12 per cent favoured marriage at the cost of career. It means only a small proportion of the respondents preferred either career or marriage. But 68 per cent wanted both career and marriage. It means, the sample, under investigation, was interested in combining both career and marriage. The respondents did not want to adopt any extreme side. The respondents further clarified that career and marriage could not be set against each other. With better understanding and tolerance on the part of the husband and wife, both career and marriage can be managed successfully. To quote Sandhya (1992): "Career and gainful employment for women do not carry any longer social stigma and inhibitions. It is no longer a question of either job or marriage but the reconciliation of the two roles (24)" To sum up, this section has tried to know the attitudes of working women towards employment. The aim was to know the degree of commitment of working women towards career. The respondents clearly indicated that for them career was as important as marriage.

Working Woman and Marriage and Family

Marriage and family constitute the fundamental institutions of human society. A woman's role and status are integrally connected with marriage and family. Changes in the structure and organisation of marriage and family will have a deep and lasting influence on the changing role and status of woman. In the following pages an effort is made to examine whether or not the working woman is becoming modern in terms of secularism, rationalism, liberalism and egalitarianism, with regard to issues connected with marriage and family. The issues discussed are as follows:

1. Marriage as a sacrament: attitudes towords divorce
2. Marital status and employment
3. Mate selection
4. Love marriage versus arranged marriage
5. Dowry
6. Widow remarriage
7. Family Planning
8. Joint family / nuclear family.

Marriage

Marriage among the Hindus is a sacrament, a holy union of two souls. As a sacrament, it is supposed to purify the human body, soul and mind and qualify for Moksha. It is obligatory and compulsory for every Hindu, both male and female, to go through the rites of marriage. As a sacrament, marriage among Hindus is irrevocable. The parties to the marriage cannot dissolve it at will. They are bound to each other for life. Even death cannot separate the twin souls. The death of any one of the spouses disqualifies the other spouse from remarrying. But the widower can remarry, preferably a virgin girl. However, his remarriage with a widow will disqualify him from participating in any ritual and deprive him of social and ritual privileges accorded to married spouses on occasions of marriages of their children and kith and kin.

The concessions provided to a widower are not extended to a widow. The wife is supposed to be bound to her husband even after his death (Kapadia, 1958: 168) Remarriage of a widow was taboo, a sin.

With the advent of modernisation, the institution of marriage among the Hindus has been undergoing changes. It is losing some of its ritual characteristics gradually. There are trends of divorce and widow remarriage seen in the last few decades. Our assumption is that by and large Hindu marriage continues to retain its sacramental character; divorce is not socially accepted. But, widow remarriages are taking place. However, widow remarriages are not a common feature. The traditional opposition and taboos are nevertheless on the decline.

TABLE V.11

Marriage among Hindus is a Holy Union of Two Souls, Divorce Cannot be Granted Under any Conditions. Do You Agree?

Response	*Frequency*	*Percentage*
Yes	70	20
No	280	80
	350	100

From Table V.11 it can be interpreted that 80 per cent of the respondents did not agree with the statement that marriage among Hindus was a holy union of two souls. A majority stated that marriage among Hindus has lost its religious and spiritual character. It is becoming relatively a social institution. Husband-wife relationship should be based on mutual understanding, trust and confidence and not on spiritual basis.

Our findings in this regard totally negate the findings of Inderjeet Kaur (1983) who found that a majority of the respondents believed in marriage as a sacrament (P32). However, a majority believed that marriage occupied a central place in the life of the Hindus. The husband-wife relationship cannot be, and should not be, easily dissolved. But in the case of 20 per cent of the respondents, marriage among the Hindus was a sacrament. They believed that marriages are made in heaven.

In order to know the importance of marriage among the Hindus it was attempted to know under what conditions divorce could be allowed for the husband or wife.

TABLE V.12

In Your Opinion Under What Conditions Should Divorce be Allowed for Husband and Wife?

Item	*Frequency*	*Percentage*
Extreme conditions of maladjustment and unbearable conditions	210	60
If the husband marries a second wife	105	30
If the husband turns out to be unfaithfull	35	10
	350	100

In response to the question: In your opinion under what conditions should divorce be allowed for the husband and wife. " 60% of the respondents reported that under extreme conditions, divorce may be granted to the husband and wife. In case the husband took a second wife divorce could be demanded. This indicated that 30% of the working women believed that marriage occupied a critical place in their life. They were not in favour of divorce under normal conditions.

Mate Selection: Choice of Life-Partner

Studies conducted on changes taking place in the

institutions of marriage and family have shown that there is an increasing tendency among modern youth towards making an independent choice in the matter of life-partner (Uplaonkar (1998), Sethi (1976), Kaur (1983), Ross (1961)) But still the trend is not well documented by empirical evidence. Our assumption is that the desire of youths for independent choice with regard to life partner is well in conformity with the wishes of parents and elders.

The degree of freedom given to young men and women, especially women, is an indication of the social recognition accorded to them. In the traditional Indian society the family primarily constituted the basis of social life. Recognition was accorded to the individual as a member of the family and not apart from it. Thus the individual functioned more as a member of the family than an individual self. Marriages were arranged by the parents, guardians or relatives. Neither the boy nor the girl was consulted.

The elders' decision was final. Parents and Kin-members played a significant role in selecting, negotiating and arranging the marriage, and not the parties bride and groom. Marriage was not considered as primarily an affair of the boy and the girl who were getting married but as an event which involved the entire kin groups of both spouses. It was being used as a means for strengthening already existing relationships or for creating new alliances; but in any case the decision to marry a particular person rarely rested with the boy or the girl (Vina Das, 1975: 72)

With the advent of modernity in terms of formal education, science and technology, white-collar jobs, provision for women's education initiated a process of differentiation between the society and the individual. The individual was beginning to identify himself / herself as an entity in himself / herself within the society. This is not to suggest that modern youth are against the power and authority of the parents and the family. What they want is a certain amount of autonomy for self-choice in conformity with the ideals of the joint family. According to Ross (1961: 252) modern youth exhibited a tendency for free contest and increasing decision-making for themselves. Venkatarayappa (1973: 185) found that the groom was given a chance to select and choose his bride, though subject to the approval of the parents. Ishwan (1968: 72) too found that young men wanted to see their brides before marriages, and the bride was sometimes even so bold as to glance up at the young man she was being engaged to. In the following pages an attempt has been made to analyse the attitudes of working women towards mate selection in terms of freedom of choice and love marriage.

TABLE V.13

Who should Take the Decision for Settling Wards' Marriage?

Item	*Frequency*	*Percentage*
Parents	32	9
Parent with self	203	58
Self choice	115	33
	350	100

An examination of the responses, as seen in Table V.13, indicates that 58% of working women, under the study, wanted their wards to form an independent opinion about mate selection, but at the same time expected them to seek approval from their parents. It clearly showed that working women neither wanted to have total control on their wards nor were ready to grant indiscriminate freedom to decide for themselves (wards).

Love Marriage/Arranged Marriage

It is generally believed that modern youth tend to prefer love marriage as against arranged marriage. Studies by Giriraj

Khanna (1978) Kapur (1970) and Giriraj Gupta (1976) have corroborated the hypothesis. But available research also indicates that not withstanding modern changes, educated men and women tend to favour arranged marriage. Uplaonkar (1998) in his study "Rural Youth in Modern India" found that modern youth neither believed in love marriage nor arranged. They wanted a combination of both. Before proceeding to analyse the data it was thought desirable to explain the meaning of phrases "love marriage" and "arranged marriage". Love marriage is understood in the present study as a form of marriage in which boy and girl interact with each other and develop a relationship on the basis of personal likes, common interests, and finally decide to marry without considering the desires and wishes of the parents or guardians, sometimes much against the will of the parents. By "Arranged marriage", on the other hand, was understood tha the parents, guardians or kin members decide to get their children married in conformity with tradition without consulting them (Children). In the former case the power to decide would be exercised by the boy and girl, whereas, in the latter it is the parents. Arranged marriage is a traditionally accepted from of marriage practised in India for ages. Parents were, and are even today,disposed to get their sons and daughters, especially the latter, married as per customary rituals and practices.

With the recent changes in Indian society, youth are beginning to demand a space for themselves and for their voice in deciding their marriage. Ross (1961: 252) found that there was a decided desire on the part of young people to have more choice in the selection of their marriage.

The most striking change one can find is in the institution of marriage. In India, there is a slow movement away from marriage arranged by parents towards more freedom of choice. Though this change is nowhere near total freedom of choice that exists in western society, the pace of change is significant enough (Kurian, 1982: 24)

TABLE V.14

If Women are Given Full Freedom to Marry, What Form of Marriage should They Adopt?

Item	*Frequency*	*Percentage*
Love marriage	70	20
Arranged marriage	105	30
Arranged marriage with freedom of choice	175	50
	350	100

Respondents were briefed about the meaning of "love marriage" and "arranged marriage". The responses of the respondents to the question: If women are given full freedom to marry, what form of marriage should they adopt? are given in Table V.14: Data indicate that respondents neither believed in love marriage (20%) nor arranged marriage (30%). But fifty per cent basically wanted to adopt arranged marriage but with freedom of choice. When asked to clarify their stand the respondents said that the arranged form of marriage had the saction of traditions, morality, religion and society at large. But marriage should not be imposed by parents and elders. Young men and women should be given a reasonable degree of freedom to make a viable choice.

When asked about love marriage they said elders should make way for youngsters. Out of 50 per cent a majority said that love marriage cannot be accepted in India. In fact, it is important to remember that the idea of marriage based on romantic love is a recent one in human history. Giriraj Gupta, in his study "Love, Arranged Marriage, and the Indian Social structure", (1976) observed that love is considered a weak basis for marriage. As a premarital manifestation, love was thought to be disruptive element, which upset the firmly established close ties in the family, a transference of loyalty from the family, of loss of allegiance of a person, leaving the family and kin group in disdain for personal goals (p: 78). Marriages even today are arranged, though the traditional pattern has given way to the modern idea of knowing one's partner in life before tying the nuptial knot. The normative practice of seeing one's husband only after marriage has given way to seeing him before marriage. The basic values of marriage within the fold of the joint family have still retained their hold over the Hindu mind (Ramanamma & Bombawalle, 1982). In his study of Aggarwal families of Delhi, Gore (1968) found that 42 per cent of the respondents were found to hold the view that, while marriage should be arranged by the youlders, the parties to the marriage should be consulted (p. 207-209).

Our finding corroborates the views of Thomas (1964) who says that though the opportunities for love marriage are increasing, "The old convention that young men and women of respectable families ought to get married according to the wishes of their parents still sits heavily on Indian society; hence, even now, love marriages are rather the exception than the rule among the Hindus".

Worsening Status of Dowry

Most studies conducted on the influence of modernisation on traditional societies have concluded that there will be radical changes in traditional institutions and practices. To be specific, modernisation will totally abolish traditional practices like dowry. Studies by Sethi (1976), Khanna & Verghese (1978) Mehta (1970), Indiradevi (1987) have come out with the finding that employed and educated women are against the practice of dowry. Such findings need further testing by applying solid theory and methodology. Quite long back Kapadia (1958: 137) pointed out: "Education, instead of mitigating the evil, has worsened it to a scandalous proportion". The committee on the status of women in India (1974) reported that since the time of passing of the Dowry Prohibition Act of 1961, not only has the amount of dowry increased, rather it has become a necessary condition to negotiate marriage. To quote the views of the said committee: "In reality, however, dowry is considered essential to obtain a suitable match for a girl with a view to ensuring a higher standard of life for her. The increase in socio-economic inequality has been one of the most important inducements for dowry and operates at all levels of the society".

The practice of dowry is the product of Indian culture and society. It is rooted in the needs of Indian society. "The amount of the dowry is generally regulated by the social and economic status of the bride groom's father, the social prestige of the bridegroom's family, and the educational qualifications of the bridegroom. " (Kapadia, 1958: 137). According to Kurian (1982) a dowry is paid in lieu of inheritance rights of daughters. The amount varies depending on the financial status of the family and also on the qualifications of the prospective bridegroom. In case a girl is not particularly attractive, a larger amount of dowry can be a compensating factor in clinching a marriage decision. Ahuja (1982: 58) concluded that educated youth have come to believe dowry as a legitimate right. One would have expected that in the wake of modernisation, the educated youth would regard the dowry system with disfavour. But this has not come true (Anna Mathew, 1990: 88). Some studies conducted on the practice of dowry show that brides, grooms and parents themselves believe in the philosophy and ideology of dowry (Gangrade, 1979). We assume that there are definite reasons for the practice of dowry.

Social Significance of Dowry

The respondents were asked whether or not they thought dowry was necessary. The views of the respondents are given below in Table.

TABLE V.15

Do You Think Dowry is Necessary in Marriage?

Response	*Frequency*	*Percentage*
Yes	245	70
No	105	30
	350	100

Data presented in Table V.15 show that 70 per cent of the working women, under the study, said that dowry was a necessary part of the marriage ceremony, while 30 per cent said that dowry was not a necessary part of marriage. Those who believed in the dowry system were asked to substantiate their stand with reasons. The responses are tabulated in Table V.15.

TABLE V.16

Respondents' Reasons for the prevalence of dowry system

Item	*Frequency*	*Percentage*
Prestige issue	70	20
Wins respect in the family	175	50
Provides security for brides	105	30
	350	100

The importance of dowry could be understood if it is viewed in the context of the values and ideals, practices and rituals associated with marriage and family. The social status of a married woman depends on dowry both in cash and kind.

Data presented in Table V.16 show that 50 per cent said dowry won respect for the bride in the new family, while 30 per cent said that it provided security to the bride. The remaining 20 per cent said that dowry was a prestige issue. The analysis clearly shows that dowry is a social value. A further discussion with the respondents revealed that dowry depends on the educational and occupational status of the groom and his family. The parents of brides want to ensure social and economic security, higher standard of living by paying a heavy dowry. So, the rate of dowry is linked with expected social and economic security in the groom's family. A well placed boy is expected to give her a secure future, and leisurely life. It is prestigious to be the wife of a man, where a woman does not need to work (for a wage). Thus dowry encourages the belief that woman's work in the home is non-productive (Desai 1987:205). The practice of dowry, in one sense, indicates low status of woman in relation to man. But in the larger society dowry enhances a woman's status, which in turn, affects her role.

Consequences, if Dowry is Not Offered

An attempt was made to know the consequences, if dowry was not offered.

TABLE V.17

If Dowry is Not Offered What Consequences Do You Expect?

Consequences	*Frequency*	*Percentage*
Ill-treatment by in laws	168	56
Husband does not care	42	14
Exploitation in in-laws family	90	30
	300	100

Respondents were asked to say what consequences followed if dowry was not offered at the time of marriage. An examination of the responses, as presented in Table IV.17, show that 56 per cent anticipated ill treatment by parents-in-law, while 30% felt that women would be forced to undertake more manual work involving drudgery. Fourteen (14%) per cent said that if enough dowry was not brought by the bride, even the husband begins to neglect her. One high school student said, "Life in the family practically becomes unbearable". It follows from the data examined about dowry that dowry is an integral part of the institution of marriage in India.

Dowry, Education and Employment

In the following pages, it was attempted to know the influence of education and employment on dowry. To be specific, we wanted to know whether or not educated and employed women are spared from dowry.

Education

The role of education as an instrument of modernisation is well established by many studies. However, the role that education plays in bringing about change is limited by tradition. To be specific, we would like to know the impact of education on dowry. Whether or not education has undermined the practice of dowry

TABLE V.18

Do You Think the Demand for Dowry Would be Minimum if the Girl is Educated?

Item	*Frequency*	*Percentage*
Yes	180	60
No	120	40
N=300	300	100

In order to know if education played any role in minimizing the rate of dowry, the influence of education of the girl on dowry has to be taken into account in relation to factors like the groom's education and occupation, his family status etc.

It is assumed that educated women are preferred with less dowry. The reason is that educated, compared to uneducated, are thought to be an asset useful and beneficial to the family. Besides, an educated woman is believed to be an indication of family status, prestige and honour.

The respondents were asked to indicate whether or not education minimized the rate or amount of dowry. It can be seen from Table V.18 that 60% gave a positive reply, while 40% of the respondents said that education of the girl or bride does not matter much.

Of the 60 per cent who gave a positive reply, a majority said that educated girls are viewed with reference to their potentialities, abilities and skills, which compensate for dowry. But education does not abolish dowry. It only grants certain concessions. Of the 40 per cent who did not believe in the efficacy of education in influencing dowry said that since education in modern India has become a matter of certificates, it does not enhance one's status.

Without going into controversies it may be concluded that education, not withstanding its shortcomings, does influence one's attitudes and values towards dowry.

Employment and Dowry

We have seen that the education of women would influence dowry. It was also found that although education is an important factor in minimising the influence of dowry, it was not very crucial.

It is generally believed that an employed woman is exempted from the payment of dowry as her job itself becomes a source of regular income. In the following table the responses of employed women towards dowry are presented.

TABLE V.19

Do You Think an Employed Woman Would be Exempted from Payment of Dowry?

Item	*Frequency*	*Percentage*
Yes	120	40
No	180	60
	300	100

It can be seen from Table V.19 that a majority of the respondents supported the statement that employed women were not required to pay dowry at the time of marriage. A further probe revealed that in practice they had paid dowry. They said that employed women are preferred in marriage and often the heavy amount demanded or insisted upon is often exempted. But dowry is asked in a different form, such as gold, bearing marriage expenses, other accessories such as TV, vehicle, sofa set, domestic articles. It means, although there was concession in the payment of dowry is not totally swept away in the case of an employed women.

The remaining 40 per cent who denied the statement said that dowry was insisted upon as usual. It was also found that those employed women who were not prepared to or could not pay dowry had to wait for long for prospective grooms. To sum up: the study has broadly revealed that marriage among Hindus continues to occupy an important place. Respondents believed in arranged marriage with a little freedom for the girl and boy before marriage to know each other. The practice of dowry is still believed in by working women.

Changing Status of Widows

It has been already pointed out that Hindu marriage is a sacrament. The system does not make provision for divorce and widow remarriage. In the traditional Indian society, a widow was looked down upon; She was considered inauspicious. To see her in the morning was an ill omen. Her presence on any auspicious occasion forboded calamity and set-back. Being economically dependent on the members of her husband's family, she could be ill treated, abused, and cursed for any unhappy occurrence in the family (Kapadia 1978:177). The report of the committee on the status of women in India 1974 observed that on auspicious occasions widows were prohibited from participation. Widowhood among the Hindus is considered a bane and was looked down upon with disfavour and contempt. As Cormack (1960) said:"a widow in her parents' house is a burden and is treated as a servant and she gets sympathy but not much and, she is often considered the cause of her husband's death"

However, in modern India far-reaching changes have been occurring in the institution of marriage and family. The whole philosophy and ideology of man-woman relationship is changing. A new concept of womanhood is emerging. The traditional stigma and social and religious taboos and disabilities associated with widows are fast disappearing. In a national seminar on "Widow in India" a number of issues relating to widows have been discussed (Nagesh, 1988).

In the following pages it is intended to study the changing status of widows. To be specific, our aim is to analyse.

1. The attitude of working women towards changing status of widows,
2. The attitude of working women towards widow remarriage, and,
3. The attitude of working women towards remarriage of employed widows.

Our theoretical assumption is that there are changes in the status of a widow, especially an employed widow.

TABLE V. 20

Do You Think the Status of Widows is Changing in Modern India?

Response	*Frequency*	*Percentage*
Yes	280	80
No.	70	20
	350	100

The fact that an overwhelming majority of the respondents gave a positive reply shows that changes are taking place in the status of widows. Further, they substantiated their point by stating that widows are not as much looked down upon as they were two decades ago. Traditional practices like shaving the head among the twice-born caste, restriction on wearing of bangles are being given up. There are instances of widows going in for remarriages. The 20 per cent sample, which did not agree with the question said in the countryside the plight of widows continues to be sad and pitiable. On the whole, it was clear that the traditional attitudes towards widows were changing.

TABLE V.21

Do you favour Widow Remarriage?

Response	*Frequency*	*Percentage*
Yes	250	70
No	100	30
	350	100

Respondents' reactions, as shown in Table. V. 21 clearly indicated a positive outlook towards widow remarriage. Those who were not in favour constituted 30 per cent. Our finding corroborates the finding of Khanna and Varghese (1978).

Reasons for Favouring Widow Remarriage

Those who supported the proposition have advanced the following reasons.

TABLE V.22

Respondents' Reasons for Widow Re Marriage

Reasons	*Frequency*	*Percentage*
Remarriage is not wrong	85	34
Opportunity for a new life	96	30
Widows must have equal right	89	36
	250*	100

* Who favoured widow remarriage

Respondents who favoured widow remarriage have advanced different reasons for widow remarriage. While a section (34%) said that widow remarriage is not wrong, another section (30%) believed that widow remarriage provided an opportunity for a new life. Interestingly, a maximum of 36 per cent believed that remarriage provided widows an equal right. A widow commented: "widow remarriage provided a new lease of life to them". A married teacher said, "Widow remarriage prevents sexual offences". An analysis of the opinions of the sample showed there was a clear-cut verdict in favour of widow remarriage. A few respondents' narrated instances of widows with small children being ill treated, harassed and tortured by family members. Under such circumstances the widows had left their children with the deceased's (husband's) parents and moved to their (widows) own parents. Respondents also pointed out that in modern times it is better to think of remarriage than to remain a widow.

Respondents Not in Favour of Widow Remarriage

As stated in the previous section, 30 per cent (100) Respondents Not in Favour of Widow Remarriage of the respondents were not in favour of widow remarriage; 70 per cent said that widow remarriage was against the values of society, while only 25 per cent raised the issue of children. In her study, Pratima Kumari (1988:124) found that the respondents were not in favour of mother widows' remarriage. Her respondents feared that if she (widow), having children, got remarried, the latter had to suffer and her conjugal life was also disturbed. A respondent said: "A widow can be accepted in marriage only in the nuclear family". To conclude, widows have to face the problem of children and marital adjustment if they decided to remarry.

Prospects of Remarriage of Working Widow with and without children

The employment status of a widow makes a good deal of difference for her remarriage. Here our aim was to know if employment status made any difference for her remarriage in case she is without children or with children.

TABLE V.23

In Your Opinion What are the Prospects of Remarriage of a Working Widow, with or Without Children?

Degree of Prospects	*With Children*		*Without Children*	
	Frequency	*Percentage*	*Frequency*	*Percentage*
1. High	175	50	210	60
2. Medium	140	40	105	30
3. Low	35	10	35	10
	350	100	350	100

X^2=8. 18, d. f. =2, significant (p>0. 05) (table value=5. 99)

Respondents' attitudes to the question: 'In your opinion, what are the prospects of remarriage of a working widow, with or without children", as shown in Table V.23 indicate that a working widow with (50%) or without (60%) children had high prospects of remarriage. There is every possibility of a working widow being preferred in remarriage. A widow's working status acts as the chief source of motivation for remarriage. The proportion of those who believed in the medium degree of prospects of remarriage of a working woman with (40%) and without children (30%) was substantially more. It could be concluded that a working widow with or without children has greater prospects of remarriage in her life. It can also be concluded that employment does make a difference to the degree of prospects of remarriage of a widow.

Planned Parenthood

The philosophy of Planned Parenthood or the small family norm is the product of the 20th Century. Revolutionary changes have occurred in the attitudes, values and outlook of the people about standard of living, education and occupation, health of parents and their children. The philosophy of small family norm has become part and parcel of the middle and upper class culture in urban areas. Children by choice and not by chance are the theme of the Planned Parenthood movement. Rural people continue to believe in more children and the large family. Nevertheless, the philosophy of the small family norm has affected their values in recent decades through Govt. schemes and programmes (Uploankar, 1998). The acceptance of the small family norm in any society, especially in a traditional society like the Indian, depends not only on the significance of modern values such as standard of living, health and housing, but also exertion of traditional values such as desire for male children. Our assumption is that limitation of family size depends to the extent a couple has male children. Vanita Srivastava (1978: 24) hypothesized:

1. That working women would have smaller families.
2. That they would start the use of family limitation methods much earlier after marriage and would also use them more effectively.

3. That they would have more knowledge of family planning methods.
4. That the ideal size of the family preferred by them would be smaller.

Importance of a Male Child in India

The desire for children is a universal sentiment. There has been a consistent preference for male children. Female children were avoided as far as possible. According to Hindu scriptures the Sanskrit word "Putra" is one who saves the father from going to hell (Kapadia, 1958: 167). Besides, it was believed that a son would continue the family lineage and support parents in their old age. Female children were, and are to some extent, considered a source of misery and sorrow. Ross (1961) points out that a woman's position as a "mother of sons" gives her authority in the household. But in modern society with the spread of education the attitudes of parents towards preferring the male to the female have undergone changes. A certain degree of equality is visible. But the desire for the male child persists even today. The main focus here is not to know whether or not working women have adopting family planning, but to know whether or not they are influenced by basic traditional values, say, the desire for a male child. This section deals with:

1. Belief in family planning
2. Advantages of family planning and
3. Significance of children especially male.

Belief in Family Planning

Studies conducted on the attitudes of educated and working women have clearly shown a positive desire for the small family (Mishra, 1993: Kumar, 1988; Jain, 1998).

The Table V.24 containing data on the belief in family

planning clearly shows that a majority (77%) of them indicated their belief in family planning, while 23 per cent did not. It indicated our sample's belief in modern values.

TABLE V.24

Do You Believe in Family Planning?

Response	*Frequency*	*Percentage*
Yes	270	77
No	80	23
	350	100

Advantages of Family Planning

The respondents were further asked to explain what advantages they perceived about family planning. The responses are presented in the table below.

TABLE V.25

In Your Opinion, What are the Advantages of Family Planning?

Advantages	*Frequency*	*Percentage*
Helps to have a small family	54	20
Secures a higher standard of living	108	40
Health of parents and children is protected	108	40
	270	100

The advantages of family planning, as believed by the respondents, clearly indicate their perception of benefits of family planning. For example, 80 per cent of the respondents (40% each) emphasized two major benefits, that family planning secured a higher standard of living and it protected the health of the parents and their children. The remaining 20 per cent said that family planning helped in having a small family. Viewed from any point of view it could be concluded that a majority of the working women, under the study, believed in family planning as they were convinced of the uses and benefits of family planning in terms of higher standards of living and health for the family. Our findings agree with the findings obtained by Sangeeta Mishra (1993).

Disbelief in Family Planning

Out of 350 respondents, 80 or 23 per cent, who did not believe in family planning gave conservative opinions like, 'it is against God's will; god will provide food, shelter and clothing for all'. This section of respondents might have been drawn from rural background and lower class.

Ideal Number of Children Desired

With the advent of industrialisation, urbanisation and modernisation, a new philosophy of "investment in man" is growing among the middle and upper classes. There is a tendency to develop human quality. Obviously educated parents tend to limit their family size. In the following paragraphs it is attempted to know as to how many children are desired by our sample viz., working women.

TABLE V.26

Ideally, How Many Children Should a Working Woman Have?

Ideal No. of Children Desired	*Frequency*	*Percentage*
One	65	25
Two	172	65
Three or more	33	10
	270	100

The data (see Table. V. 26) show that the ideal number of children desired by the majority of the sample (65%) is two. A small sample of 25 per cent was interested in one child, while only 10 per cent of the working women in our study were fond of three or more children. A discussion that followed the interview revealed that those who had a desire for two children said that in view of the rising costs of living in urban areas, it was difficult to rear and bring up more children. More or less, the respondents who preferred the one child norm gave similar views. Those who preferred three or more children said that to limit the number of children to one or two children is risky and dangerous if the couple has only male or female children. To conclude, the majority of the respondents wanted to have a small family.

Actual Limitation of the Family Size

Always there is a difference between the ideal and the actual limitation of the family size. The actual limitation of the family size depends on religious and socio-economic values associated with the birth of male and female children. For example, in Hindu society, the birth of a male child is considered very important. A couple without male children becomes the target of criticism and humiliation; we therefore, assume that the actual size of a family to be limited depends on the number of male and female children borne by the couple.

Preference for Male Children

Studies conducted on the preference for male children have arrived at different conclusions. According to Sangeeta Mishra (1993:140) female respondents were of the opinion that the birth of a male child brought more joy than that of a female child. The birth of a male child enhanced the position of women in the family circle and hence they celebrated the birth of sons with more joy in comparison with that of their daughters.

The traditional desire for male children on the one hand, and contempt for female children on the other is fast disappearing in the wake of modernisation. The emerging trend is in favour of both male and female children. As high as 60 per cent of the respondents (see Table V.27) indicated that they wanted both males and females. But a section of the

TABLE V.27

In Your Opinion, Should a Working Woman Stop Bearing Children, if She Has

Item	*Frequency*	*Percentage*
Only male children	105	30
Both male and female children	210	60
Only female children	35	10
	350	100

respondents (30%) indicated its preference for only male children. Their contention was that male children are not as much a problem as females. The fact that only 10 per cent wanted to have only female children shows that only female children are not preferred. The sample's preference for both male and female children shows that working women continue to prefer males, but females are not disliked. It may be inferred that the actual size of the family to be limited depends on whether a couple has both male and female children. Employment seems to have created tensions and fears in the minds of working women.

The Changing Status of Joint Family and Working Woman

The joint family as the basic and predominant form of family in India has existed since ancient times. It is based on intimacy, mutuality of interests', strong primary group control and mutual assistance in times of need. Family interest and goals are always held high in relation to individual members. The status and role of woman in the joint family is generally low. She has fewer rights, little power and authority, while more duties and obligations. On the other hand, a woman in the nuclear family is accorded higher status and greater role. Our assumption is that the status and role of a working woman depends on the extent to which the joint family is making way for the nuclear family.

Sociologists are divided in their opinion about the changing pattern of the joint family in the context of modernisation. Kapadia (1956), Desai (1955: 1973) and a host of others have argued that the joint family has not undergone any basic changes under the impact of changes under the impact of modernisation. According to Kapadia (1956), what the young demand is the reorientation of the relationship between the older and the younger members and not the rejection of the joint family. In his study of Agarwal families of Haryana, Gore (1968) came to the conclusion that although limited changes were appearing in the joint family system, nevertheless, by and large, the joint family had remained intact.

On the other hand, Goode (1963) and Ross (1961) have concluded that the joint family in urban areas is transforming itself into a nuclear family. For example, Ross says: "A silent social transformation is taking place in the Indian family with educated woman breaking away from accepted family traditions and family controls and looking beyond their homes for self-expression" (1961:8). The controversy regarding the changing pattern of the family in India has failed to be resolved because of the precise definition of the joint or nuclear family. It is unfortunate that although a lot of research has been done on joint family, nevertheless, it is not clear as to what constitutes a joint or nuclear family. For example Gupta defines joint family as "A group composed of a number of family units living in separate apartments of the same house who eat food cooked at one hearth, share a common income and common property, are related to one another through agnatic Kinship such as man, his sons, grandsons, or set of brothers, their sons and grandsons " (1974:104). However, sociologist like Desai (1955) and Shah (1973) have stressed more sharing of kinship obligations than income or property.

According to Srivastav (1980:90) a joint family is an

arrangement in which two or more married couples, besides other relatives, live together under the same roof and, share a common kitchen". But the definition does not make clear whether two married couples refer to two married brothers. It may as well refer to parents and married son.

According to Sinha "the Joint family is characterised by the presence of three or more generations of lineal descent who share properly, residence etc" (1987:47). But in modern India a joint family need not have three generations. If two married brothers live together and share common expenses then it may be classified as a joint family.

The above definitions do not bring out the critical dimensions of the joint family system. Basically the joint family is a relationship between married brothers who share common income and responsibilities. Venkatarayappa has given a relatively better definition of joint family. According to him "The joint family is that family in which more than one married son lives with the parents sharing a common habitat, kitchen and labour". This also includes a number of married brothers living together with parents (or without them in case they are dead) and sharing a common social life and economy (1973:186). In the present study the joint family is understood as defined by Uplaonkar (1998:81): " a group where two or more married brothers live together by pooling their income and sharing family responsibilities, obligations, and commitments. It may include parents, uncles, sisters or daughters or widows and other near or distant relatives". In short, a joint family is a joint family in so far as married brothers live together in the same household. The moment they establish their separate households, the joint family ceases to be a joint family. The general understanding of nuclear family is that it is a group composed of husband, wife and their unmarried children. But this definition does not hold true in the context of India. A nuclear family is understood as a group composed of husband wife, and their unmarried children all staying in an independent household. But it may include a parent or unmarried sister or brother. Power and authority are vested in the son, not in the father. But nuclear or elementary family is not totally detached or disconnected with the parent family. The nuclear family is joint as far as its kinship obligations are shared by its members. A brother staying with his wife and children may be obliged to share common kinship obligations such as marriage of a sister or brother or parents' treatment in a hospital.

Working Women and the Joint Family

Studies conducted on the attitudes of working women towards the joint family have come out with the conclusion that working women tend to establish a nuclear family. According to Ross (1961:50), as the phenomenon goes on, it is expected that the individuals, especially women, would find it preferable to establishing independent nuclear homes to living in large families which entail adjustment with many members of the family. Srivastava (1978:87) also found that a large proportion of the respondents preferred to live in nuclear families. The basis of the assumption that working women were less likely to be living in joint families is that as a consequence of their employment these women would become more independent in their outlook. They might like to have a greater say in family matters and that might make them less tolerant of their in laws. The study revealed that their families composed of husband, wife, their issues and one parent was more common among working women (p. 89). It has been already stated that out of 350, 200 or 57 per cent of the respondents had been living in joint families, while 43 per cent had been living in nuclear families. Similar findings were also obtained by Kaur (1983:39). In the following paragraph it is sought to know why 57 per cent of the respondents lived in joint families.

TABLE V.28

You Said You are Staying in a Joint Family; What Made You Opt to Stay There?

Reason	*Frequency*	*Percentage*
Living together is strength	40	20
Educate and marry youngsters	80	40
Look after the aged and disabled	80	40
	200	100

Table V.28 provides the data with regard to the respondents' reasons for staying in a joint family. Out of 200 respondents 40 per cent said that there were young brothers-in-law and sisters-in-law (husbands' brothers and sisters) who were to be educated and married. Some said their family had heavy expenses, which require pooling together of income from different sources. The other 40 per cent were mainly concerned with the welfare of the aged and disabled. Some even said that looking after and taking care of their parents-in-law was their bounden duty; if they did not discharge that duty properly they would incur the wrath (shrap) of their ancestors and gods. In the case of 20 per cent of the respondents the joint family sysmbolised unity, and strength. Respondents elaborated the point stating that their parents-in-law did all the sundry job works like purchases, payment of bills, domestic chores, taking grand children to schools and bringing them back. In short, working women felt that they were relieved of many responsibilities in joint families, which otherwise they would have to do. To conclude, a majority of the respondents believed in the system of joint family for its benefits and usefulness.

Reasons for Staying in Nuclear Family

The emergence of the nuclear family in modern society is a stark sociological reality. Under the impact of industrialisation and urbanisation, the large traditional joint family is yielding place to small and independent elementary families. In the following pages we have tried to study the reasons, which prompted working women to establish a separate household.

TABLE V.29

You Said You are Living in a Nuclear Family. Please Tell Me the Reasons for Living in a Nuclear Family Away from the Parent Family

Reasons	*Frequency*	*Percentage*
Greater freedom to live one's own life	45	30
Provide a higher standard of living	90	60
Cannot adjust with other family members	15	10
	150	100

An analysis of the responses, as shown in Table V.29, brings out the respondents' reasons for staying in nuclear families, 60 per cent said that they were more interested in giving a better standard of living, good education, food, shelter, health and security to themselves and for their children. But 30 per cent of the respondents wanted more freedom, independence and liberty in life. Only 10 per cent said that they could not adjust with a number of members in a joint family. It could be deduced that working women living in nuclear families were conscious of higher standard of living. Respondents said that in a joint family we cannot develop our children as per our aspirations and plans. Respondents also felt that one can be free and independent in making decisions in the nuclear family. It could be concluded that those who preferred a nuclear family were status-seekers. The emergence of the nuclear family is an indication of the quest for higher status and role by its members.

Interaction between Joint Family and Nuclear Family

Research available on the changing forms of the joint

family in India in the last five decades has not come to any unanimous conclusions. One group of sociologists has held that under the impact of modernisation the joint family system is breaking down. Others hold that the joint family is a rural phenomenon while the nuclear family is an urban factor. In other words, with the growth and expansion of industrialisation and urbanisation, the joint family will be replaced by nuclear family. But studies do not support that view. Gore's (1968) study has shown that the respondents believed in the joint family. Our data clearly reveal that joint families and nuclear families even in urban areas can coexist together. The investigations made by I.P. Desai provide us with a different framework for understanding the interdependence of the elementary and extended family in India. In the following pages it is attempted to examine the mutual relationship and interaction between the joint family and the nuclear family.

Respondents living in joint and nuclear families were asked to give answers to a set of questions about mutual help and co-operation.

1. Do you help joint/nuclear family members in times of family needs such as education and marriage of younger brothers and sisters?
2. Do you help your parents/brothers/sisters-in-law etc. during illness?
3. Do you help and co-operate with your family members (joint or nuclear) in life-cycle ceremonies? Their responses are given below.

Respondents living in joint and nuclear families have indicated that although they were living in separate households, sometimes in distant towns and cities, they maintained regular contact with each other and never cut off relations.

TABLE V. 30

Do You Want to Help Members Living in Joint/Nuclear Families? If Yes, How?

Ways of Interaction	*Joint Family*		*Nuclear family*	
	Fr	*%*	*Fr*	*%*
1. Help financially in times of family needs like education, marriage	20	10	30	20
2. Help in times of illness etc	40	20	60	40
3. Participation in life-cycle	140	70	60	40
Total	200	100	150	100

X^2=31.48, d.f. = 2, significant (p>0. 05) (table value=5. 99)

It can be seen from Table V.30 that 70 per cent of joint family and 40 per cent of nuclear family members wanted to cooperate with each other in conducting and organising family events such as birth, cradle-ceremony, marriage and death. Separate living did not prevent them from participating in family functions. It did not lead to antagonism and hatred. Ten per cent and 20 per cent of joint and nuclear family members, respectively, wanted to help each other in times of difficulties by way of service and financial assistance. One nuclear family respondent said: "I have sought the help of my mother-in-law during delivery and medical treatment".

Similarly, 20 per cent of joint family members and 40 per cent of nuclear family members wanted to help each other in times of illness and financial crisis. It could be concluded that though both types of families are structurally different from each other, they are functionally close to each other. The emergence of nuclear the family has strengthened joint family and the continuation of the joint family has protected the nuclear family. K. Ishwaran (1982) in his article "Interdependence of the Elementary and Extended Family" has clearly brought out the mutual dependence of both forms of families. It follows from the discussion that working women in our study living in nuclear families, although they enjoy a greater role and status, are not totally last to joint family values.

6

Status and Role of the Working Woman in Family

The concept of status and role of woman has been defined in terms of rights, power, authority and responsibilities, duties, obligations. We have tried to analyse the status and role of the working woman in the family in terms of:

1. Position as perceived by the respondents in the family
2. Freedom to act
3. Involvement in decision-making the family
4. Sharing of domestic responsibilities by other members of the family
5. Problems of adjustment in the family.

Our aim is to know to what extent progressive changes were taking place in the status and role of the working women, under investigation, with reference to the five dimensions of status and role in the family. A number of studies have attempted to analyse and measure the changes taking place in the status and role of the working woman (Srivastava, 1978; Indiradevi, 1987; Talwar, 1984; Kapur, 1970, 1974; Mishra, 1993; Lalitha Devi 1982). But none of them has taken into consideration the necessary dimensions that are critical to measure the status and role of the working woman. Besides, there are differences of opinion about the findings. Kapur (1973) found that although working women were allowed to take part in the decision-making process in the family, her decision was not final. Usha Talwar (1984), in her study "Social Profile of Working Women", has tried to analyse the role of working women in decision-making. Her observation led to the point that gainful employment raises the position of woman and increases her role in decision-making within the family. It is necessary, therefore, to study the changing role and status of the working woman in the family with reference to her role as decision-maker.

1. Position of Working Woman in the Family

Family organization forms the basic care of a given society's sexual division of labour, marital norms and a system of control over resources, rights, duties and privileges of the members. Employment of woman in white-collar jobs with a steady income and security of job has significant consequences for her role and status in the family in particular, and in the society in general. A woman's status in the family would be

TABLE VI.1

Working Woman's Perception Regarding Her Position in the Family

A Working Woman, How Do You Perceive Your Position in the Family in Relation to Other Members?

Relationship	*Perception of Position in %*			*Total*
	High	*Equal*	*Low*	
1. Husband	—	40(140)	60(210)	100(350)
2. Parents-in-law	20(70)	40(140)	40(140)	100(350)
3. Brothers-in-law (Employed)	20(70)	60(210)	20(70)	100(350)
4. Others	80(280)	20(70)	—	100(350)

X^2=37. 32, d. f. = 6, Significant (p>0. 05) (table value = 12. 6).

Note: Figures in parentheses are actual frequencies.

definitely related to whether she is engaged in gainful economic activity or not. According to Gore (1968) a woman's lower status in the family is related to her exclusion from economic activity. Consequences of woman's employment to the family have been delved into by many researchers (Wood, 1975, Mehta, 1976). In the following paragraphs, it is attempted to analyse how working women in the sample perceived their position in the family.

A higher status and role are traditionally accorded to males in family. They are vested with power, authority and privileges to control and regulate the activities of the family and its members. On the other hand, female members are supposed to be subordinate to the male members. By virtue of their higher social status men have always acted as heads of the family. According to David G. Mandelbaum (1970), "In his role as husband, man should always be the superior, the initiator, the receiver of deference from his wife. Commonly, she renders the expected gestures freely, spontaneously, and in full, as part of her expected womanhood, not out of feelings of duress" (74). The wives are expected to be modest, submissive and dutiful to their husbands and other members in the family, although, a woman acquired higher status with the attainment of motherhood. However, she was not accorded the status as head of the family. According to the traditional norms of society a husband is expected to be an authoritarian figure, whose will should always dominate the domestic scene; the wife should regard him as her master and serve him faithfully. The husband is superior, the wife is subordinate.

However, the status and role of educated and employed women is changing from subordination to one of equality. Sociologists like Raj Mohini Sethi (1976) attempted to study whether or not modern women felt equal to men. A similar attempt is made here to analyse how working women perceived their relative position in the family. Our aim was to know whether or not employment of woman has altered her status with her husband, parents, parents-in-law, employed brother-in-law etc. Our assumption is that employment has improved a woman's status in relation to her husband, parents-in-law etc., but her relative status, nevertheless, broadly conforms to the traditional frame of status and role. Let us analyse the data. An analysis of the data presented in Table VI.1 shows that no single employed woman in our sample perceived her relative position as being higher than that of her husband. However, 40 per cent felt their position to be equal to their husbands', while 60 per cent thought that their status was lower than that of their husbands'. A majority of them said that, however high the status a working woman may enjoy in her office, she can never claim higher status in the family than her husband. A middle-aged lady said, " A husband is a husband, whatever status she (the wife) may enjoy in her office". In a similar attempt, Mohini Sethi (1970:93) found that Indian women still believed in the natural superiority of men to a large extent. However, employed women were treated by their husbands with respect and honour. An interesting but important development was that 20 per cent felt their status was higher than that of their parents and parents-in-law. The respondents said that their parents, or parents-in-law themselves acknowledged their (respondents') enhanced status in many day-to-day activities. Similar was the reply from those 40 per cent who felt that they were on an equal footing with their parents / parents-in-law. However, for 40 per cent of the sample, their parents / parent-in-law were always adorable. Employment of woman could not make her either equal to them or higher.

Of the total sample, 20 per cent claimed higher status in comparison to their employed brothers-in-law, while 60 per cent of the sample felt their status equal to theirs. But 20 per cent thought it still, low vis-à-vis the other members of the family. All in all, the majority (80%) felt their status was higher than it could have been but for their employment. From the above analysis the following conclusions may be drawn.

1. The majority of the working women in our sample believed that their status was lower than that of their husbands. Nevertheless, there were symptoms of change in the case of 40 per cent of the sample who believed their status to be equal to that of their husbands.
2. When asked to rank their status in relation those of their parents / parents-in- law, 20 per cent said high, 40 per cent equal and 40 per cent low. It shows that employed women were ranking themselves higher than their parents / parents-in-law probably because they were not employed in white-collar jobs.
3. The respondents also ranked themselves either equal or higher in relative to other members like employed brothers-in-law.
4. Compared to other members of the family like distant relatives, the respondents believed themselves higher. It could be concluded that employed women are claiming a higher status and role as due to them.

2. Working Women and Freedom

The status and role of women depends on the degree of freedom accorded to them in the family and society. On the other hand, restrictions on freedom deprive one of the right to equality. Thus freedom and equality go together in a democratic setup. It is attempted to analyse here the status of working women in terms of degree of freedom accorded to them.

To know the degree of freedom given to working women, the following question was asked "where do you keep your salary every month"? It can be seen from Table VI.2 that 40 per cent of the respondents handed over their pay pocket to their husbands, while 20 per cent handed it over to their parents / parents-in-law. It is a significant development that 40 per cent kept their salary with themselves. The 40 per cent of the respondents, who handed over their salary to their husbands, said that they had no freedom to keep their salary with themselves. Respondents had to seek permission from or at least intimate to the husband if they (respondents) wanted to spend any amount from their salary. Promilla Kapur (1970) also found a similar trend. For example, in the study of educated working women a large majority of the respondents reported that they were not allowed to spend even their self earned money the way they felt like spending and had to hand over their pay to their husbands or in-laws"(p. 66).

TABLE VI. 2

Where Do You Keep/Deposit Your Salary Every Month?

Item	*Frequency*	*Percentage*
With the Husband	140	40
Parents/Parents-in-law	70	20
With Oneself	140	40
	350	100

It means employment in the case of 40 per cent of the respondents does not seem to have given a greater degree of freedom and independence. Similar views were expressed by 20 per cent of the sample who handed over their salary to their parents / parents-in-law. The fact that 40 per cent of the respondents kept their salary with themselves showed that they enjoyed a greater degree of freedom. The respondents further said that there was perfect understanding between them and their husbands about financial matters. The respondents themselves contributed their salary as per the requirements of the family. During the discussion it emerged that husbands and parents-in-law believed that they had a natural right not only on the working wife but also her salary. A question was casually asked: What would happen if the respondents did not pay their salary to their husbands? The respondents said that in that case they (husbands/parent-in-law) would not allow them to stay in the family. On the whole, 60 per cent of the respondents did not have the freedom to keep their salary with themselves. But 40 per cent of them were accorded a greater degree of freedom.

Working Woman and Freedom to Spend

The degree of freedom accorded to working women in the family was further analysed by asking a question whether or not they had the freedom to keep back certain a portion of their salary for on personal consumption, gifts and presents to relatives, friends and colleagues or spend on parents' health or on one's own brothers' or sisters' education or marriage. The question is: Is or is not a working woman free to spend

TABLE VI.3

How Free are Working Women to Spend/Pay from Their Salary on the Following Items?

Items	*Degree of Freedom in %*			*Total*
	Very much free	*Just free*	*Not free*	
1. Clothes, jewels, costumes for personal consumption	50(175)	30(105)	20(70)	100(350)
2. Domestic Appliances	50(175)	15(51)	35(124)	100(350)
3. Savings for Children	65(250)	25(90)	10(10)	100(350)
4. Personal LIC, F.D. etc	40(140)	40(140)	20(70)	100(350)
5. Presents, gifts for relatives, friends	35(122)	25(123)	30(105)	100(350)
6. Parents' health, own brothers, sisters', education or marriage	20 (70)	30 (105)	50 (175)	100(350)

X^2=333. 6, d. f. = 10, significant (p> 0. 05) (table value=18.3)

Note: Figures in parentheses are actual frequencies.

on people who are not related to her husband's family? In her study, Sandhya (1992) observed that her respondents had freedom to save money for their children's education and marriage. But that does not mean that a working woman is free in terms of personal autonomy. In the following paragraphs, an attempt is made to know how far the working woman is free to spend on friends and relatives and save money for her children.

The responses of the respondents, to measure the degree of freedom enjoyed in the family to spend a portion of their salary on certain needs, are presented in Table VI.3.

1. Freedom to spend on jewels, clothes, costumes, and personal requirements.

   Analysis of the data shows that 50 per cent of the respondents said that they were very much free, 30 per cent free to a limited degree and 20 per cent not free to spend on personal requirements such clothes, jewels etc. This means that half of the respondents felt that they had a relatively greater degree of freedom. This means the salary earned by the respondents did not belong to them.

2. Freedom to spend on domestic appliances.

   The respondents were asked to indicate how free they were to buy domestic appliances required for cooking, etc as and when needed. It can be seen from the data that again 50 per cent of the respondents were free to a great extent to purchase domestic appliances. But the remaining respondents felt they had restrictions on spending on such items. Husbands and parents-in-law expressed dissatisfaction over expenditures on what they thought were unnecessary items. But the respondents said they wanted to use the latest appliances.

3. Freedom to save for Children.

   Whatever savings are made by the working women will remain as property with the family. The majority of the respondents (65%) said that they were given relatively more freedom to save money in various deposit schemes. Only 10 per cent were constrained to invest in their children's future. The husbands and other family members evidently had a vested interest in the children's progress and career.

4. Freedom to Invest for personal Security – LIC, FD etc.

   As can be seen from the data, the maximum 40 per cent had a considerable degree of freedom to invest in LIC, FD, and UTI etc. The remaining respondents, it appears, were not encouraged. The reason they advanced was that their husbands thought that there was no need to invest in personal deposits. It was observed that there were differences of opinion cropping between the employed women and their husbands on the one hand and parents-in-law on the other, over the issue of expenses and savings.

5. Freedom to spend on presents and gifts for relatives and friends.

   The working woman, by virtue of her employment, faces certain unexpected problems. As an employee, her colleagues expect her to participate in and attend marriage, birthdays, and anniversaries. It involves expenses. Similarly relatives and friends expect working women to attend marriages and traditional functions and present costly gifts. Expenses on such occasions exert pressure on one's salary. A maximum of 35 per cent had just a little or some degree of freedom to spend on such occasions. But the remaining 30 per cent had no freedom to spend on such occasions.

Most respondents said that they had to seek permission or intimate to their husbands/parent-in-law. Often the presents, such as sarees, watches, domestic appliances etc, had to be shown to the husband and parents-in-law. In short, the working women, under investigation, were not free to spend a part of their salary as per their will and wish.

6. Freedom to spend on parents' health / education or marriage of own brothers and sisters.

Women workers had practically no freedom to spend from their salary on the medical treatment of their own parents or bear the expenses of education or marriage of their own brothers and sisters. For example only 20 per cent of the respondents were quite free to share any expenses from the parents' side. But 50 per cent were not at all free to share any financial commitment from their parents' side. The respondents said that their husband's family members thought that a working woman's income belonged to them and her parents or kith and kin had no right over it. But the respondents did not concur with such a view. They said their parents had an equal right on their income.

It could be concluded from the analysis of the above data that employment has not, as expected, enhanced status in terms of freedom, which is an important component of equality.

3. Involvement of Working Women in Decision-making

Decision-making in the family is a critical element in the status of family members since it involves the allocation of resources and the distribution of roles within the family. In order to measure the role of women in the decision-making process, it is necessary to assess their influence on all the family decisions.

The right to decision-making is an important and integral part of infra-family democracy. A person's status and role depends on the extent to he or she is involved in decision-making. Indira devi (1987: 123) defines decision-making as an activity process by which a course of action is consciously chosen from available alternatives. Mohini Sethi (1989: 40) in her article "Status and Power of Rural Women" operationalises the concept of decision-making power through the woman's perception of who mainly decides and is in control of the affairs of the family. Decision-making involves the possession of power. Emerson (1964: 297) conceptualized power as the ability to influence others i. e. to withhold rewards from and/ or to apply punishment to others.

Involving women in decision-making or allowing them to take their own decisions means recognition of their right and power. In our thesis, decision-making is understood as consultation, discussion and taking into confidence. We have studied the following issues:

1. Attitudes of husband and parents-in-law towards working women's ability to take independent decisions.
2. Degree of involvement of working women in the decision-making process.

Involvement of Women in Decision-making in Traditional Family

In the traditional joint family, male members, as heads of the family, had the right, authority and power to organize, control and direct the family activities. Women were not only expected to be involved in decision-making but were thought to be not qualified and fit to make decisions. Manu, the law-giver, said women were unwise, short-tempered and fickle- minded. It was also believed that they could not make independent, responsible and mature decisions, as they are highly emotional and sentimental. In the traditional joint family the position of the wife was governed by un-egalitarian values. For example, Dube (1955: 141) observes that in an ideal home the final say in all matters connected with the family is always with the husband. However, a wife's position in decision-making normally improved with the passing of time. As she became a senior member of the family she was being invited to give her opinion.

Gore (1968) points out that seniority in age or in generational status would give a woman a higher symbolic rank in relation to certain men in the family but generally male superiority in the Hindu family is supported by tradition and man's right of property. In modern society the traditional prejudices and stereotypes associated with her nature are considered outdated and meaningless. Education has provided her the ability to think and act responsibly. Employment is not merely a source of income; it is a source of power and security, too. With employment women begin to experience a sense of independence. According to Lalitadevi (1982: 4) "Once education and economic freedom came together, they activated one of the basic wishes of an individual – wish for recognition, i. e. status. " Employment also develops appropriate ability to spend money judiciously.

Working Women and Decision-Making

Several researches have led to the conclusion that due to their economic contribution, working wives have greater a say in family affairs. Heer (1958) has stated that both in the working class and in the middle class, the working wife exerts a greater influence in family decision-making. Similarly, Kliger (1958) has shown that the working mother influenced family decisions on major purchases, loans, savings and investments to a great extent.

Glueck and Glueck (1954) study showed that working wives dominated family affairs. In India Indiradevi (1987) has devoted a separate chapter on decision-making. Similarly, Srivastava (1978) Usha Talwar (1984), Lalitadevi (1982) have done a lot of research on Women's employment and decision-making in the family. Our assumption is that employed women have a definite say in the decision-making process in the family, especially, in the nuclear family. But the husband continues to dominate the family.

TABLE VI.4

Do You Think Working Women Can Take Responsible Decisions in Their Life?

Degree of Decision-making	*Fr*	%
To great extent	200	55
To some extent	80	25
Never	70	20
	350	100

Since ages women have been socialized to believe that they are inferior and inefficient. They are always dependent on men. This kind of inferiority complex was supposed to be rooted in their personality. But their perception is changing. As education, especially higher education, develops a self-awareness of oneself, a new identity is evolving. Educated women are beginning to believe that they are like any other individual. Thus a new social image is developing among educated women. Employment has further strengthened their individuality and autonomy. An employed woman has greater freedom in family decision-making, greater latitude in spending family income. An employed woman is a more competent decision-maker. In families with working women, the family decisions would be changed from being male-dominated towards being more egalitarian joint decisions (Lalitadevi, 1982: 45).

Changing Perception of the Respondents

An attempt was made to know whether or not the traditional perceptions of women were changing. The respondents were asked: Do you think working women can take responsible decisions in their life? An examination of the data, as shown in Table VI.4, revealed that a majority of 55 per cent said their perception was changing to a great extent, while 25 per cent said to 'some extent'. Just 10 per cent gave a negative response. In other words, a majority of the respondents were beginning to realise that they could also take responsible decisions in life. The change in their perception is an indication of their growing status.

Perceptions of the Family Members about Women's Ability to take Responsible Decisions

To study the changing status and role of the working woman, it is necessary to know if there are any positive changes in the perceptions of the family members such as the husband, parents-in-law about her ability to take responsible decisions in life. Information collected in this regard is presented in Table VI.4.

TABLE VI.5

Do You Think There is a Considerable Change in the Attitude of Your Family Members Viz. Husband, Parents-in-Law Towards the Ability of Working Women to Take Responsible Decisions?

Family members Working	*Woman's Ability to Make Decisions*			*Total*
	To a great	*To some*	*Nil*	
Husband	50(180)	30(105)	18(65)	100(350)
Parents-in-law	35(150)	20(70)	45(130)	100(350)

X^2=31. 88, d. f. = 2, significant (p>0. 05) (table value=5. 99)

Note: Figures in parentheses are actual frequencies.

Changes in the perceptions of family members about the ability of working women to take responsible decisions are clearly seen in the data presented in Table VI.5. For example, 50 per cent and 30 per cent of the respondents felt that changes were taking place in the attitudes towards working women's capability to take responsible decisions to a great extent and to some extent, respectively. The respondents explained that husbands of the working women have realised that educated and employed women are as competent and efficient as men are. Modern forces like education, science and technology, mass media, have initiated new channels of socialisation. A respondent said: "No society can afford to underestimate women any longer now".

Interestingly, similar changes in the attitudes of parents-in-law were not seen in the data. A maximum of 35 per cent and 20 per cent of the respondents said that changes in the attitudes of the parents-in-law about the ability of working women to take responsible decisions had taken place to a "great extent" and to "some extent" respectively. On the other hand, 45 per cent of the respondents did not believe that working women could take any responsible decisions in their life. The respondents reported that their parents-in-law were very conservative. It can be concluded that there are positive changes taking place in the family members view about women's abilities and capacities.

Involvement of Working Women in Family Decision-making

A final attempt was made to analyse the role of the working women, under investigation, in the family decision-making process.

It appears that working women by virtue of their education and employment, would exercise a significant influence on the actions of the family members. To a question, if respondents were involved by family members in family decisions, as many as 60 per cent and 30 per cent said that their husbands consulted them 'very often' and 'often', respectively. It means, by and large, the working women were taken into confidence by their husbands, while taking any decision. When asked to cite examples, many respondents gave instances of purchasing gold, jewelry, gifts etc. where both husband and wife together did the shopping. Wood (1975: 42) study showed that working women participated in decisions concerning such issues as their husbands jobs, shifts in residence and their children's schooling. It is clear that working women in our sample were involved by their husbands in decision-making.

TABLE VI.6

How Often are You Consulted by Your Family Members Such as Husband and Parents-in-Law, While Family Decisions are being Taken?

Family Members	*Degree of Consultation*			
	Very often	*Often enough*	*Never*	*Total*
Husband	60(210)	30(105)	10(35)	100(350)
Parents-in-law	40(140)	30(105)	30(105)	100(350)

X^2=28, d. f. = 5 significant (p>0. 05) (table value=5. 99).
Note: Figures in parentheses are actual frequencies.

Data also suggest that as far as decision-making was concerned, there was not much interaction between working women and their parents-in-law. In many cases the mother-in-law was domineering. A maximum of 40 per cent of the respondents had frequent interaction with the mother-in-law in purchasing new clothes for festivals, functions etc. Another 30 per cent of the respondents were consulted on few occasions. The remaining 30 per cent said that they were practically never left out of consultation on several occasions. The reason was that the mother-in-law was jealous of daughter-in-law's employment. On the whole, it could be concluded that the working women, in our sample, were involved, consulted, take into confidence or otherwise in decision-making.

4. Working Women and Sharing of Domestic Responsibilities

Traditionally, men and women were assigned different occupations and responsibilities. Men were expected to work in the fields and earn the livelihood for the family. On the other hand, the duties assigned to women were those of cooking, serving food, washing clothes and cleaning utensils. Men were ranked higher than women in the system of division of labour. S.C. Dube's (1955) pioneering work on the Indian village community throws light on the traditional division of labour between the sexes. Women's work centred round the tasks, which are internal to the household. On the other hand, men's work centered round strenuous jobs, both on the domestic and farm front and work roles involving the outside world.

(1) Changing Work-Norms

With the advent of industrialisation and urbanisation work-norms based on sex and division of labour are changing. A number of jobs and occupations have been acquiring a neutral status. Women are increasingly taking to white-collar jobs. Employment of women has affected relationships in the family. Husband and wife, parents-in-law and daughters-in-law have to redefine their relationships in the context of women's employment.

(2) Consequences of Woman's Employment on Family

Studies conducted on the consequences of Woman's employment on family have shown that a wife's employment will compel the husband to share domestic responsibilities. "As a consequence of a longer working day and dual responsibilities, the working wife may appeal to her husband to help in her household work", "As a consequence of their economic support their husbands are more likely to help them in their household work" (Srivastava, 1978: 87). According to Indiradevi (1987: 92), "The employment of women creates a situation for the emergence of joint roles compared to the segregated roles". The employed status of the wife gives her an important place in the power structure of the family and she begins to have an equalitarian role in the family. Her voice becomes influential in home management (Blood and Hamblin, 1968: 182-87). However, it is still not clear to what extent husbands of working women are involved in sharing household duties. For example, it is not clear if husbands of working women share domestic chores, such as cooking, serving and washing equally. This may be true in western countries. According to Young and Wilmot (1973) husbands of working women do all sorts of domestic chores including cooking, washing and cleaning. Thus, there is a greater degree of equality between husbands and working wives in the West. But the same is not true in India. Prakash Rao and Nandini Rao (1982: 213) report that neither employed nor non-employed mothers get any help from husbands. M. Hanumantha Rao (1990) in his article "Employment of the Wife, and Husbands' Participation in House-Work", attempted to understand the areas of house-work in which the husbands of Working Women participated. He concludes, the traditional sex-specific division of labour does not appear to have changed very much in the families of working women. There is a rigid demarcation of what is woman's work and what is man's (455).

In this section our aim is to find out to what extent the respondents feel that there is equality between husband and wife in sharing domestic responsibilities. The phrase "domestic responsibilities" is understood as cooking and serving food, cleaning utensils and washing clothes, daily shopping, looking after guests and relatives, maintenance of accounts and payments, taking care of the children.

First, we wanted to know how often the working women were being helped by family members in their domestic chores.

TABLE VI.7

How Often the Following Members Extend a Helping Hand in Your Domestic Chores

	Members Degree of help			
	Very often	*Often enough*	*Rarely*	*Total*
1. Husband	—	40(140)	60(210)	100(350)
2. Mother-in-law/ Sister-in-law	40(140)	40(140)	20(70)	100(350)
3. Servants	50(175)	40(140)	10(35)	100(350)

X^2= 87. 1, d. f. = 4 significant (p>0. 05) (table value = 9. 49)
Note: Figures in parentheses are actual frequencies

Table VI.7 indicates that husbands' help in managing domestic works was minimum, as only 40 per cent of the respondents said that husbands cooperated often. But 60 per cent of the respondents said husbands rarely helped. It means husbands' cooperation was not readily forthcoming. But in the case of mothers / sisters-in-law, the respondents reported that they gave co-operation very often (40%) and often enough (40%). Broadly speaking, 80 per cent of the respondents received help from their mothers / sisters-in-law. Interestingly, working women in the sample seem to have depended more on servants as 50 per cent and 40 per cent reported that their servants helped them very often and often enough, respectively. Other studies conducted on working women have shown that working women received more help and cooperation from cooks and maid servants. Our study has clearly brought the fact out that husbands generally do not help in domestic matters. In an other attempt we have tried to know the contribution of family members in sharing the domestic responsibilities of working women.

TABLE VI.8

In Your Day-to-Day Domestic Chores What is the Contribution of Your Family Members?

Domestic Chores	*Family Members*			*Total*
	Husband Mothers/	*Sister-in-law/*	*Self Servant*	
1. Cooking and Serving food	20(70)	60(210)	20(70)	100(350)
2. Cleaning and washing	—	40(140)	60(210)	100(350)
3. Domestic purchasing	50(175)	40(140)	10(35)	100(350)
4. Looking after guests and relatives	40(140)	60(210)	—	100(350)
5. Accounts and payments	30(105)	70(245)	—	100(350)
6. Care of Children	40(140)	30(105)	30(105)	100(350)

Variance Test: F=0. 565, d. f. = 10, significant (p>0. 05) (T. value=18. 3)

Note: Figures in parentheses are actual frequencies

1. *Cooking and Serving Food*

With regard to cooking and serving food to family members, especially men, the majority (60%) of the respondents reported that it is a woman's job. Only 20 per cent of the respondents pointed out that men also can do cooking and serving food. The remaining 20 per cent believed that cooking and serving food can be the responsibility of both men and women. A doctor respondent remarked: "Why cooking and serving food be the sole responsibility of women only?" Of the 60 per cent respondents the majority said: "in case men started cooking and serving food, they themselves felt insulted". Indian society does not accept men doing cooking and serving. However, a few respondents said that their husbands did the cooking and serving, even cleaning of utensils, if they (women) fell ill or were advised bed rest during the monthly course or delivery of child. To conclude, as far as cooking and serving of food is concerned husbands do not share the responsibility. According to Ramanamma (1979: 107) " In a majority of cases, when the wife asked the husband to help her in the household work, he felt his superiority questioned by the wife. To him doing household chores was beneath his dignity. Other members of the family belittled a husband whose wife was employed outside the house and expected him to help her with the cooking and of utensils. Tension thus developed in the life of the wife.

2. Cleaning and Washing

Cleaning utensils and vessels, washing clothes and sweeping the house have been women's duties. But employed women, because of paucity of time, cannot do cleaning and washing. Maid servants are increasingly appointed to help. It could be seen from Table 7 that as many as 60 per cent of the respondents took the help of servants, while 40 per cent either did the job for themselves or took the help of mothers-in-law. But none of the husbands did the job of cleaning and washing. Employment of women has relieved them from domestic drudgery but has not brought equality. Cleaning and washing continue to remain woman's duties.

3. Looking after Guests and Relatives

Looking after the guests and relatives is the responsibility of the family. In India 'Athiti Satkar', looking after or caring for the guest, visitors, and relatives is the foremost duty of the family. It is believed that guests are the very embodiments of gods. Wealth, peace and harmony thrive in families where guests are honored and looked after. Our data in this regard show that the chief responsibility of looking after the guests and relatives belonged to women (60%), while the men shared a part of it (40%). But a further probe into the responses revealed that the entire family should be engaged in entertaining the guests. The respondents said that there were certain duties like marketing or taking around the sight-seeing should be done by men alone. Preparation of food etc., were the responsibility of women. It could be stated that looking after the guests and relatives is the responsibility of the entire family and not of any particular individual.

4. Domestic Purchases

Sixty per cent of the respondents reported that their husbands generally did all daily and monthly purchases such as foodgrains, oil, tea powder, soaps etc. and daily items like vegetable, eggs, meat etc. However, 20 per cent of the respondents said that women must also do domestic purchases. The remaining 20 per cent said that both husband and wife should do domestic purchases. It is clear that domestic purchasing is being shared by both husbands and wives.

5. Maintenance of Accounts and Payment of Bills

Generally, maintenance of family accounts and payments is done by the husbands. But educated and employed women are also sharing the responsibility. As per our data, 50 per cent of the respondents expected their husbands to do it, while 30 per cent of them wanted wives to do the job. Only 20 per cent expected both husbands and wives to share the work. It is clear that financial matters are dealt with by husbands, although wives are taking interest in it.

6. Care of Children

There was a time when rearing of children was the sole responsibility of the mothers. But in modern society rearing children has become a complex process. Admission of children to school, coaching them at home etc require scientific skills. Data suggest that 40 and 30 per cent believed that wives and husbands should take care of children, respectively. But 30 per cent of the respondents felt that both husband and wife should take care of the children. On the whole, according to respondents, caring for children is being shared by husbands and wives.

To sum up this section: Both husbands and wives shared family difficulties, problems and responsibilities. But husbands never did the job of cooking and serving of food. It is still believed as the major duty of the wives.

In a similar study Shashi Jain (1998 : 222) came to the following conclusion : "Cooking they (working women) had to do themselves in most of the cases. It shows that working women are, by and large, responsible for their household duties and get assistance only from time to time. In fact they have to worry about their households. Usha Talwar (1984 : 88) too found that husbands participated in many tasks of house keeping, except cooking and serving food. In joint families other members assisted in cooking and serving food. But in nuclear families husbands did not expect their wives to serve food, but served for themselves. It was also observed that working women could not do justice to the traditional role as house wife as far as domestic work and housekeeping was concerned. This was also observed by the Report Status of Women in India (1974 : 85).

5. Working Woman and the Problems of Adjustment in the Family

Employment of women is a double-edged instrument. It has advantages and disadvantages to the employed woman herself and the entire family. In this section an attempt is being made to analyse the problems of adjustment of working women with the members of the family. When the working woman goes to work, she has to combine work at home and office which is bound to create stresses and strains. It is very difficult to strike a balance between the two: Studies conducted on the effects of woman's employment have held differing views. Some studies have come to the conclusion that employment of woman does not affect her traditional role of wife and mother (Kapur, 1970; Ranade and Ramchandran, 1970; Srivastava, 1973; Kaur, 1983). There are others who hold the view that employment of woman creates role-conflict (Hate, 1969 : 97; Mahajan, 1966; Joshi, 1973). Our assumption is that a working woman, by virtue of her education and employment, develops a sense of social and economic superiority and tends to develop problems of adjustment.

Working Woman and Superiority Complex

TABLE VI.9

It is Often Believed that a Working Woman Tends to Look Down Upon Non-working Members of the Family: Do You Agree?

Response	*Frequency*	%
Agree fully	189	54
Agree partly	91	26
Don't agree	70	20
	350	100

It has been already stated that a working woman develops a sense of superiority. Data gathered from our respondents reveal that a maximum of 54 per cent of the sample fully agreed with the statement that a working woman tended to look down upon non-working members as inferior. Another 26 per cent also partly agreed with the statement. It means clearly that the employed woman segregated herself from non-employed members. It was only 20 per cent of the sample who did not believe that employment developed a sense of superiority over others. Data suggest that employment of woman produces class differences.

Husband-Wife Relationship

A harmonious relation between husband and wife is an important indicator of an employed woman's status. A working woman, because of her employment, begins to assert her independence and equality. She may refrain from open confrontation. But she will not accept the husband's superiority. Promilla Kapur in her two studies "Marriage and the Working Woman in India" (1970) " Marriage and Sex", (1973) fund that more and more educated women had started challenging the conventional and traditional husband-wife relationship in which there was the husband's absolute superiority and dominance over the wife and in which the wife was supposed to surrender herself completely to the will of her master and even suffer in silence. This was indicated by the fact that the percentages of those women had increased considerably who disapprove of a relationship of "husband's superiority, wife's inferiority" and of husband's dominance, and wife's submission". A study by Rao and Rao (1973: 175) concluded that "the traditional asymmetric husband-dominated family is changing towards a more symmetric or syncretic type of family where the mother is employed, indicating a major role-conflict resulting in a chain of consequences". Rama Mehta's (1976) study found that the boys, though influenced by more modern values, were still conformists in many respects. They expected of their wives the traditional submissiveness to their authority and subordination to the family. They seemed to have changed very little in their views regarding the place of the wife in the home in spite their being a near-equal contributors to the family earnings".

Working Woman and Marital Relations

TABLE VI.10

Do You Think that There Could be Differences of Opinion between the Working Woman and Her Husband on Family Issues? If Yes, specify the issues

Issues	*Yes*	*No*	*Total*
1. Not sufficient contribution of salary for home expenses	75(262)	25(88)	100(350)
2. Not paying enough attention to the needs of the husband	60(210)	40(140)	100(350)
3. Neglecting overall family interest	55(192)	45(158)	100(350)
4. Not taking enough interest in children	58(203)	42(147)	100(350)

X^2=35. 04, d. f. = 3, significant (p>0. 05) (table value=7. 81)
Note: Figures in parentheses are actual frequencies.

Before analysing the data, let us explain the meaning of

marital adjustment. The phrase marital adjustment is understood in this study as defined by Promilla Kapur (1974) "a state of accommodation in marital relationship between husband and wife which is characterised by a tendency in them to resolve conflicts and solve problems, to come to a mutual agreement on important issues of married life, and also by an overall feeling of happiness and satisfaction with marriage and with the marriage-partner" (p. 21). Obviously, when there is no understanding, agreement and consensus on matters of married life and family, conflicts begin to develop between them. We also assume that employment is one of the factors, and not the only factor for maladjustment between husband and wife.

A glance at Table VI.10 clearly shows a certain degree of difference of opinion on family issues between the husband and the wife. Let us analyse the data.

1. Not Contributing Sufficient Salary to Family Expenses

Data show that as high as 75 per cent of the respondents said that there were differences of opinion about what portion of salary to contribute family expenses. They (respondents) said the husbands expected them to contribute a greater portion of their salary to family expenses, while they (husbands) themselves either saved their salary or spared for their relatives. Some others said: "The husbands wanted to run the family with the wives' salary," some respondents said: 'Their husbands apprehended that they (the wives) might be sparing a portion of the salary for their (wives) parents and kith and kin". It was observed that the respondents were not happy with their husbands with whom they (wives) had regular arguments/skirmishes over this issue.

2. Not Paying Enough Attention to the Needs of Husbands

Employment of woman obviously means that the woman has to spend long hours outside the family in connection with her job. When she comes back home from her place of work to home, she herself is tired and exhausted. Similarly, the husband is tired, too. Either she has to take extra pains to offer a cup of tea to her husband or to take the services of servants. In any case, the employed woman cannot pay personal attention to her husband as much as a non-employed one does. As a result, the inter-personal relations between the husband and the wife are likely to sour. An overwhelming majority (60%) of the respondents said that a working woman cannot attend to the needs of the husband. They said office duties consume more than 70% of their time and energy. By the time they reach home they are totally exhausted. However, 40 per cent of the sample said that employment of woman does not become a source of tension, provided there is understanding between husband and wife. They (respondents) said both husband and wife have to redefine their expectations and develop maximum patience, tolerance and endurance. In conclusion, it may be said that employment of woman makes life more routine-like, mechanical and timetable oriented. When the husband comes back from work, there could be tension if both husband and wife are tired after the day's work (Giriraj Khanna, 1978).

3. Neglecting Overall Family Interests

Employment is not only a source of income but also a way of life. The working wife is compelled to neglect family interest while attending office functions. Fifty five (55%) per cent of the respondents felt that they could not take care of family interests, fully. For example, they could not participate in Kinship programmes and functions. But 45 per cent said there was not much difficulty in attending the overall family interests. It required a little special effort to maintain a balance between family and office obligations.

4. Not Taking Enough Interest in Children

Rearing children in modern society is a full-time job. It

means upbringing on scientific lines. In a family where both husband and wife are employed, upbringing of children is left to the servants and teachers. Parents have no time to look into the needs of their children. Constant attention of the mothers and her physical presence are considered essential to provide a healthy psychological environment for the development of a child's personality. Data gathered by Srivastava (1978) showed that employment gave a feeling to the mothers that they were neglecting their children. Dhingra (1972) has also found that more than half of the working women of his sample felt tremendous difficulty in looking after the health and general upbringing of their children in a manner in which they wanted to do. Our data also reveal that 58 per cent felt that since they could not take care of their children, there were arguments and counter arguments between husband and wife. The wife pleaded her inability to look after the children due to her dual role of home and office. But the husband was not satisfied with his wife's plea. However, a maximum of 42 per cent said that there was no difficulty in training their children. Of course, servants and tutors assisted in shaping up the children. But the parents themselves took care to pay personal attention. Usha Talwar (1984) also found differences of opinion between husband and wife over family matters. It could be concluded that in the case of a majority of the sample, lack of personal attention to children developed differences of opinion between the husband and the wife.

Studies have reported that a working woman always hangs between her family and office. Kapur's detailed study (1970) and Narula's survey (1967) of career women in middle class families strongly indicate that an educated working woman's attitude towards herself and her employment was ambivalent. On the one hand, she works because of the various socio-psycho-economic satisfactions that she derives out of work. On the other, she dislikes it and resents it because of the stresses and strains caused by the job as also because of the conflicts and tensions created within herself on account of her own inability to look after her husband, home and especially the children. It could be concluded that working women in our sample were tension ridden about their duties and responsibilities of family and office. At least our study shows that working women could not strike a balance between the home and office.

Working Woman and Adjustment with the Mother-in-law

Traditionally, the relationship between the mother-in-law and daughter-in-law has been characterised by one of conflict and quarrel. The mother-in-law in relation to the daughters-in-law was vested with power and authority to run the family smoothly.

According to Ross (1973: 114) "It is perhaps the potential drama entailed in the mother-in-law daughter-in-law relationship that has caused it to be one of the most publicized of all family relationships. Traditionally a mother-in-law was able to wield more naked power over her daughter-in-law". The mother-in-law and daughter-in-law were, and are even now, jealous of each other. The mother-in-law always wanted to rule over the daughter-in-law by controlling her son, while the daughter-in-law wanted to protest against the highhandedness of the mother-in-law by taking her husband into confidence. The son is always in a state of dilemma; he is torn between his mother and wife. The mother-in-law, however, lost her power over her daughter-in-law, as the latter became a mother of sons. In this section we would like to study the role of the employment of the daughter-in-law in establishing harmonious relations with the mother-in-law. We assume that since the traditional values are very strong, employment of the daughter-in-law will create rifts, tension and conflicts.

TABLE VI.11

It is Believed that the Working Woman Cannot Adjust with Her Mother-in-Law: Do You Agree? If Yes, Give Reasons

Reasons	*Yes*	*No*	*Total*
1. Non-acceptance of mother-in-laws superiority	85(297)	15(53)	100(350)
2. Economic Superiority	72(252)	28(98)	100(350)
3. Tendency to dominate others	55(192)	45(158)	100(350)
4. Tendency to separate from parents-in-law	82(287)	18(63)	100(350)

X^2=98. 8, d. f. = 3, significant (p>0. 05) (table value=7. 81)

Note: Figures in parentheses are actual frequencies

To understand the impact of employment on the daughter-in-law mother-in-law relationship, the following question was asked: 'It is believed that a working woman cannot adjust with her mother-in-law. Do you agree? If yes, give reasons'. The responses are presented in Table VI.11.

1. Non-acceptance of Mother-in-Law's Superiority

We have already stated that the mother-in-law has the right to dictate terms to the daughters-in-law. She expects obedience and subordination from them. But we have also seen that the educated and employed woman develops a sense of independence. She considers self-respect and personality development as her life-goals. Education and employment promote a sense of ego. Clash of egos breeds a of revenge. As the employed daughter-in-law becomes revengeful, she begins to disregard and disrespect the mother-in-law. It can be seen from the data that 85 per cent of the respondents said that they were not ready to accept the traditional superiority of the mother-in-law. Husband's fear of snub may force them to keep their lips shut. But tensions in inter-personal relations continue to erupt now and then.

2. Economic Superiority

Social status involves power and authority. Economic power gives the daughters-in-law a sense of superiority so as to dictate terms to others, including the mother-in-law. Conflict between the two begins take place, as the mother-in-law would never accept the daughter-in-law's economic superiority. Seventy two (72%) per cent of the respondents said economic superiority is the cause of tensions between the mother-in-law and the daughter-in-law. However, 28 per cent did not think that social tensions could be arising out of the daughter-in-law's employment, provided the daughter-in-law gave respect and regard to the mother-in-law. In short, employment results in ego clash.

3. Tendency to Domineering over Others

Employment has several dysfunctions or disadvantages to the family and its members. The employed daughter-in-law, by virtue of her economic superiority, begins to assert her power and authority through protests and confrontations with the members of the family. She expects equality with her husband and mother-in-law, if not a higher status. Fifty-five (55%) per cent of the respondents admitted that employed daughters-in-law begin to dominate on others. But 45 per cent did not agree and said that a daughter-in-law is still traditional in her outlook and values, and tend to respect family members. It could be concluded that although there is a tendency among working daughters-in-law to assert their new status, it was also observed they were for compromise and mutual tolerance.

4. Tendency to Separate from Parents-in-Law

Even in the traditional joint family, the daughter-in-law has always desired to establish her separate family. It was due to family pressure and public opinion that she stayed in the joint family. Employment of the daughter-in-law gives a special push to the idea of living separately. Besides, the high economic status of employed spouses creates class differences and might become the cause of separate living. Eighty-two (82%) per cent said that there was a tendency in working women to establish a separate household separate from the joint family. Eighteen (18%) per cent, however, said that the daughters-in-law are safe and secure in joint families.

To sum up: in this chapter we have tried to analyse the changing status and role of the working woman in the family by taking into account four aspects. Viz.,

1. Freedom to spend salary,
2. Involvement of working woman in decision-making process,
3. Sharing of responsibilities by family members, and
4. Problems of adjustments in the family - with the husband and mother-in-law.

Our analysis has shown that employment has not brought significant changes in the status and role of the working woman in the family. For example, the working woman does not have the freedom and liberty to spend a portion of her salary as per her wishes. She is consulted on many matters of the family. But the final decisions are taken by the elders and male members. In the case of domestic responsibilities, the working woman seemed to be overburdened. Of course, she is assisted by servants and female members. The husband makes little contribution, if anything, in sharing the domestic responsibilities. Cooking and serving of food continue to be the major responsibilities of the working wife. Some are helped by female cooks. Finally, the status and role of the working woman was analysed with reference to her relational adjustments with the members of the family. There were differences of opinion between husband and wife over family matters. There were quarrels and skirmishes between the two over mutual rights, duties and expectations. Similarly, the working daughter-in-law and the mother-in-law could not pull on. Both tried to assert their superiority over each other. As a result there was no harmony in the family.

From our data it could be said that employment of woman has brought about changes in the status and role of woman when compared to the same in the traditional society, but she is far from being on a footing of equality with her husband. The employed woman has not yet struck a balance between home and office. Her status and role are yet to crystalise and be articulated. Jyotsna Rajvanshi (1991) has this to say: " In the face of all this evidence we can conclude that patriarchy in the intra-family structure largely remains intact, in spite of the woman's external higher status and participation in economic activities. Her position is precarious in this situation where she must work and at the same time, conform to an image of ideal womanhood in which employment was regarded as immoral for women. She has to fulfill all the duties concerning household organisation because home is regarded as the primary responsibility for a woman, if she fails to perform her primary role, husband / family members oppose this situation. Thus education and employment have brought about only a marginal structural or qualitative change in this sphere "(p. 226).

7

Status and Role of the Working Woman in Office

THE STATUS AND ROLE OF THE WORKING WOMAN IN OFFICE

The working woman in modern India has to face new challenges and obstacles to acquire and establish a new status and role in office which has been traditionally a preserve of men. The term "office" has been defined in a variety of ways. In simple words, it can be described as a place where some business is carried on. But this is an inadequate definition of office. The term "office" in our study is not defined or understood as a place where clerical work is done. It is understood in a broad sense. It means a place where groups of people work together to achieve a common goal. The term "office" is understood as an organization, which denotes a structure of duties and activities necessary for the conduct of business. The organization serves two important functions:

1. It defines the relationship between the sub-functions so as to co-ordinate the efforts of people in the accomplishment of the overall task effectively and efficiently, and,
2. Organization serves as a pattern of ways in which a number of people relate themselves to each other in the planned and systematic accomplishment of a

complexity of tasks. This objective tends to emphasize personal relationships and the human element to a great extent.

The term 'office', in the sense of an organization, refers to a group or an association of individuals working in a pre-structured manner for achieving pre-determined common goals. The term 'office' in our study includes schools, colleges, clinics, banks, and administrative offices etc. , where employees are ordered in a system of stratification, namely, as high and low.

The working woman has to face three problems in order to adjust herself with the office.

1. The working woman has to play two roles at a time viz. , wife, mother, and employee.
2. The Office (gainful employment) has been, and continues to be, dominated by men. That means, she has to work in a men's world.
3. Working woman, compared to men, is new to office culture. Office is formal organization with rules, regulations, procedures and modes of work.

Office culture includes:

(1) Office duty as per rules, regulations and procedures of the organization (school, college, hospitals, bank etc.)

(2) Office functions such as get-togethers, farewells, marriages, etc. , and

(3) Union activities.

The working woman has to be inducted into office culture. Perhaps it requires generations to develop acclimatization to traditions of Office.

Ultimately, it all depends upon the working woman how she overcomes the obstacles. A number of studies have been conducted on the emerging status and role of the working woman in office (Ramanamma, 1979; Kapur, 1974; Talwar, 1984; Nayar, 1988; Jain, 1989; Kala Rani 1976; Bhoite, 1987; Chakraborthi, 1978, Mishra, 1993; Lalitha Devi; 1982). However studies by Lalitha Devi, (1982); Ramanamma, (1979;) Promilla Kapur, (1974), Kala Rani, (1976) and Anuradha Bhoite, (1987) are worth mentioning. Lalitha Devi (1982) sought to enquire into the performance of women in offices i.e. how well do they perform their role in equality with males and how comfortable do they feel in office? The author used the following variables for measuring the status of a woman worker within the office.

1. Respect from superiors (male)
2. Respect from colleagues (male)
3. Respect from subordinates (male)
4. Organization's, work related activities, and
5. Job satisfaction

According to the author, the respondents found no difficulty in adjusting with men staff in office. Hence, there was no role conflict. Promilla Kapur also found similar trends. Kala Rani's study (1976) found that employment of wives increased chances of marital conflict to some extent (P. 180). In her study "Women Employees and Rural Development". Anuradha Bhoite (1987) found that their respondents experienced role conflict. In the present chapter we want to explore whether or not the working woman faces any problems of adjustment in office. We have taken the following factors into account.

1. Working women and interpersonal relations with men and women colleagues.

2. Working woman and efficiency.
3. Attitude of male workers towards female workers as perceived by the latter.
4. Attitudes of higher officers, colleagues, and subordinates towards working women .
5. Working Women and active participation in office functions, and
6. Working women and union activities.

Let us Analyse the Data

1. Working Woman and Interpersonal Relations

Employment of woman means working with men and women in an organization. It entails a certain degree of positive attitude on the part of both men and women towards each other. Both have to come out of traditional gender inhibitions and apprehensions.

TABLE VII.1

In Your Opinion, with Whom Do Working Women Frequently Go for Lunch and Coffee, and Chitchat During Leisure in Office? (in %)

Friends	*Very Frequently*	*Frequently*	*Never*	*Total*
1. Men	10 (35)	60 (210)	30 (105)	100 (350)
2. Women	60 (210)	30 (105)	10 (35)	100 (350)

X^2=195, d. f. = 2, significant (p>0. 05) (table value=5. 99)

Note: Figures in parentheses are actual frequencies.

According to Table VII.1, the working women, under investigation, tended to have more social contact with women workers than with men workers, as 60 per cent of the respondents very frequently had gone for lunch, coffee or engaged in chit chatting with women as against only 10 per cent with men. It means clearly that women workers preferred to establish interpersonal relations with women more than men. This could be interpreted as a sign that there was a socio-psychological gap between men and women workers. When asked, out of 210 respondents who had very frequent contact with women workers, a majority (50%) said that they felt safe, secure and comfortable with women and felt free to talk personal and family problems. On the other hand, they could not converse the same way with men. They also said that there should always be an "arm's distance" between men and women, whether in the family or in office.

However, 60 per cent of the respondents had gone for lunch or coffee or had social contact with men workers as against a maximum of 30 per cent with women. They argued that it was necessary for working women to have some formal contact with the men with whom they had to work in office. It means our respondents wanted to have formal relations with men workers as far as office was concerned. But they wanted women-workers to share their (respondents) confidence and trust. Interestingly, 30 per cent of the respondents never had any contact with men, while 10 per cent never mixed with women. Two conclusions may be drawn. One, a great majority of the respondents had a maximum (very frequently) social contact in terms of going for lunch or taking coffee or chitchatting with women. In other words, our respondents preferred women as friends or peers. This exhibited a conservative attitude towards men. And two, a sizeable proportion of our respondents had frequent contact with men. By this they meant formal relations as far as office work is concerned.

2. *Working Woman and Efficiency*

Another attempt was made to measure the attitude of the working woman towards working men. Such an analysis will help us in knowing whether the respondents have a positive or negative approach towards men workers.

TABLE VII.2

In Your Opinion, with Whom Can Working Women Work Efficiently—Men or Women?

(in %)

	MoreEfficiently	*Less Efficiently*	*Not Efficiently*	*Total*
1. Men	20(70)	60(210)	20(70)	100(350)
2. Women	50(175)	30(105)	20(70)	100(350)

X^2=80, d. f. = 2, significant (p>0. 05) (table value=5. 99)
Note: Figures in parentheses are actual frequencies.

The attitudes of the working women towards men workers can be easily seen from Table VII.2. Data clearly suggest that a greater proportion (50%) of the respondents believed that they could work more efficiently with women, while those respondents who felt that they could work more efficiently with men was very low (20%). It means women workers feel they could do their job with greater efficiency in company with women than with men.

But 60 per cent of the respondents said that they could work with men with less efficiency. It means a greater proportion of working women feel they could work with greater efficiency with women than with men. To conclude: the women workers in our study believed that they could do their job much better in company with women than with men workers. This indicates that gender inhibitions are acting as a block in the interpersonal relations in the case of women workers.

Attitude of Working Men Towards Working Women

The status and role of working women depends to a great extent on how the men colleagues feel about the working woman with reference to a set of characteristics such as punctuality, efficiency, social behaviour and hard work. We would like to know how the respondents perceive the reactions of men workers towards them in office.

TABLE VII.3

How do You Rate the Performance of Working Women According to the Factors Given Below in Comparison with Men Workers?

Abilities	*Higher*	*Equal*	*Lower*	*Total*
1. Punctuality	20(70)	30(105)	50(176)	100(350)
2. Efficiency	23(80)	35(122)	42(144)	100(350)
3. Social Behaviour	20(70)	40(140)	40(140)	100(350)
4. Hard work	25(87)	25(87)	50(176)	100(350)

X^2=23. 06, d. f. = 6, significant (p>0. 05) (table value=12. 59)
Note: Figures in parentheses are actual frequencies.

First the respondents were explained the meaning of the factors or abilities shown in Table VII.3 was explained to the respondents and they were asked to give their response as higher, equal, and lower. Promilla Kapur (1974) has shown that men colleagues in office have a poor image of working women. Working women's problems at work are also multiple which are different for those who are working with men and for those who are working with females alone. A woman has not yet been accepted as a professional worker in many jobs and occupations, though she has the "right to enter" and has actually started entering into various jobs and professions. She is not yet taken as an equally efficient worker alongside of men, in spite of all the studies that have shown that "she has anequally high capability and dexterity to carry out various jobs equally efficiently and successfully as men. And her not being considered as equally efficient and capable hurts her ago immensely " (p. 68).

It is generally believed that women are emotional and

conservative. Because of family responsibilities, a woman cannot afford to commit herself to the job as fully as do men. For example, she cannot stay beyond office hours in office to attend a function or meeting. Thus she cannot enjoy a high image among men.

Respondents were asked to rate women workers' performance in office in comparison with men workers.

1. *Punctuality*

It can be seen from Table VIII.3 that 20 per cent of the respondents said that their punctuality was higher, while 30 per cent said it was equal to that of men. When asked to specify reasons, of the 20 per cent (70) a majority said that women can be more punctual at office than men as they (women) are as competent as men. Those who believed that their punctuality was equal to that of the men said that they can also attend the office in time like the men. Interestingly, 50 per cent of the respondents said that their punctuality is lower than that of men workers. The main reason, according to them, was that they had to complete domestic chores first and then attend the office. They said they could not afford to attend the office at the cost of family responsibilities. In short, women's punctuality to attend the office depended on her family responsibilities.

2. *Efficiency*

The term is understood as working with undivided concentration and sincerity. Our assumption is that the efficiency of working women, compared to that of men workers, is affected by the family. Information collected in this regard reveals that only 24 per cent of the respondents said that they were more efficient than men. It appeared that this section of the working women had a bloated self-image. They exhibited a sense of hatred against men workers. But 35 per cent of the respondents said that their efficiency in office was as high as that of men. They argued that they could manage their home responsibilities and do their office work as efficiently as men did. This section of the respondents did not undergo any role conflict. But 42 per cent of the respondents expressed the opinion that their efficiency was lower than men's. Some said because of "monthly course" (menses) they could not concentrate on their job, while others mentioned pregnancy as the reason. Still others said differences between husband and wife, parents-in-law and themselves at home caused tensions in office. On the whole women workers due to personal and family problems, could not concentrate on their work.

3. Social Behaviour

The phrase "social behaviour" is understood as mixing and interacting with men and women without sex apprehensions. But it is difficult for women to achieve a high degree of sociability. According to Promilla Kapur (1974: 69) for office women workers the most comman situation is to work with men and to have men colleagues. But even in this inevitable situation there are tensions. If she is reserved and does not mix with the men colleagues she suffers from "social isolation" at work and is labeled by her colleagues as a snobbish and too vain of her family background, marital status or official status. On the other hand, if she is friendly and nice to them and likes their company and mixes with them, she is liable to be labeled as a flirt or as a woman who is too fond of the company of men and as such could be taken advantage of. While facing these problems, she is often confused as to what should be her actual conduct. "Generally, a socially free woman is considered a loose woman. Therefore, women generally tend to maintain social distance with men. Table VII.3 shows that only 20 per cent of the respondents said that their sociability was higher than men. They argued that one's sex does not determine one's sociability. However, 40 per cent of the respondents opined that working women were as sociable as working men. They said they can be sociable without spoiling their character. But 40 per cent of the respondents strongly believed that women workers cannot be as sociable as men are. The very personality characteristics of women come in the way of their becoming sociable. It may be observed that a woman always feels insecure in the company of men. It may be concluded that working women are less sociable, compared to men. This factor affects working women's performance in office.

4. Hard Working

It means putting maximum efforts to know, study and explore the different aspects of a subject or issue. It means going into the depths of the subject. One has to take a good deal of strain to do the job. It is assumed that women workers cannot put in strenuous efforts to do a job due to personal and family responsibilities. Women are physically weak. With the attainment of marital status and birth of children, they become still weaker. Besides, family responsibilities always exert a strain on their mind. Thus women's weak physical health and family responsibilities affect their job-performance. When asked whether working women can be hardworking in their duties, compared to men, 25 per cent of them said that they are more hardworking than men. An analysis of the data collected from the respondents with regard to their attitude towards hard work shows that only 25 percent of the respondents said that they are more hardworking than men. Their main contention was that in no way are women inferior to men viewed from any point of view. It was observed that those who asserted their superiority over men were deeply hurt when the above question was asked.

One point was clear that women are beginning to assert their abilities, skills and rights. But 50 per cent openly admitted that their ability to work hard is low compared to men. Nevertheless, they (50%) said they can manage their office without any difficulty. A clerk in office said "In fact we want to be punctual and hardworking. But family responsibilities, transport etc., will act as a drag on their performance in office. It may be concluded that half of the respondents said that they can undertake any work which involves hard work. But the other 50 per cent said that they could not work as hard as men.

To sum up, working women's performance in office was measured in terms of punctuality, efficiency, social behaviour and hard work. It was found that working women's performance of office duties is affected by family responsibilities.

WORKING WOMEN AND HIGHER OFFICERS

The status and role of working women depends upon how they receive respect, honour, sympathy and co-operation from their superiors, equals, and lower staff members. According to Lalitha Devi (1982: 26), women employees did not face any problem in either receiving co-operation from their superiors' enforcing discipline on their male colleagues. However, Promilla Kapur (1974) enumerates number of problems encountered by working women with their staff in office. Napasri Kraisons Wasdi (1989) made a systematic study of "Women Executives: A Sociological Study of Role Effectiveness" dealt with the interaction with office staff. The study revealed that women executives managed very well with their staff. The status of the working woman in her office needs to be studied from different points of view.

1. Working Women and the Attitude of Superiors

TABLE VII.4

In Your Opinion, What is the Attitude of Higher Authorities Towards Working Women in Office?

Attitude	*To Great Extent*	*To some Extent*	*Never*	*Total*
1. Respect and Sympathy	25 (87)	60 (210)	15 (53)	100 (350)
2. Co-operation and mutual help	22 (77)	55 (193)	23 (80)	100 (350)
3. Differences of opinion	50 (175)	30 (105)	20 (70)	100 (350)

X^2=96. 88, d. f. = 4, significant (p>0. 05) (table value=9. 488)

Note: Figures in parentheses are actual frequencies.

Superiors

The attitude of superiors or higher authorities towards the working women should be considered a crucial factor for their performance of duties in office. In her study Lalitha Devi (1982) found that working women were respected. However, Anuradha Bhoite's (1987: 60-61) enquiry revealed that although the officers usually gave considerate treatment to the women employees, they (Officers) were unanimous in their opinion about the incompetence of women employees. The officers felt a dissatisfaction regarding the performance of working women. The officers also said that the working women have neither the ability nor any urge to do the official work properly. The officers further said that working women were more interested in their home affairs.

Let us Analyse Our Data

(1) Respect and Sympathy

Our data reveal that the higher authorities did not have a high level of respect and sympathy for working women as only a maximum of 25 per cent said that their superiors had respect and sympathy to a great extent. It means the superiors did not have a high regard for the working women. But 60 per cent of the respondents enjoyed medium level respect and sympathy from their superiors. Some respondents even said that their male superiors had a prejudice against women. While others admitted that women workers because of personal difficulties could not earn the goodwill of higher officers. It was observed that male superiors had more sympathy than respect towards Working Women

(2) Cooperation and Mutual Help

Cooperation and mutual help between officers and workers is an essential condition for the smooth functioning of an organization. The relations between officers and workers should be always characterised by an attitude of "give and take". A positive attitude between the two will develop trust and confidence. However, men and women workers, because of the sex factor, are not likely to develop a higher level of trust and confidence. According to Promilla Kapur (1974:68), "In the case of a woman's working under a male boss, the psychological problem is created by his tendency of not taking her as an efficient worker first, but that of taking her as a woman primarily. If she pays a lot of attention and appreciation and is too polite, courteous and good to him in the interest of her job, promotion or career, he is liable to take advantage of his position and official status and exploit her". A woman worker is always in a dilemma. Our data with regard to the superiors' attitude of cooperation and mutual help towards working women shows that a maximum of 22 per cent expected greater co-operation and mutual help. It means that the working women could not build up a close rapport with their "bosses". Many respondents said their superiors did not assign them any risky, responsible and confidential tasks. A college lecturer said: "Women cannot keep secrets to themselves for long, they make it public". Others said women tend to spread news. Significantly, 55 per cent of the respondents said that they did receive co-operation and help from their superiors to some extent. A majority of the respondents said that they were engaged in routine office tasks. Many respondents said they rejected promotion to administrative jobs, as it required management of men. But a significant section of the respondents (23%) said they never received any cooperation and help from their superiors.

(3) Difference of Opinion

Difference of opinion between superior officers and their subordinates are a part and parcel of any organizations. Women workers generally do not want to have open confrontation with their bosses. But differences of opinion on many grounds do crop up and operate between the two. Differences of opinion may divide the officer and worker and may gradually develop a stable communication gap. An attempt was made to know if the relations between the working women and their higher officer were strained. Data indicate that 50 per cent of the respondents felt that they had differences of opinion with the superiors to a great extent. It means they were not happy with the superiors. When asked for reasons, they said men officers had a tendency to harass women workers. Respondents complained that they were subjected to mild forms of taunts and insults. This was further supported by 30 per cent of the respondents who too expressed the view that they had bitter experiences with the superiors sometimes. Interestingly, 20 per cent of the respondents did not have any differences of opinion with the superiors. To sum up, only a small section of the working women enjoyed a high degree of respect, sympathy and cooperation from the superiors. But it also emerged that a majority of the respondents also enjoyed a moderate degree of respect and cooperation from their superiors. It can be said that a majority of the working women had a minimum level of understanding with their superiors. But it is also the case that a majority of them had occasional differences of opinion with their superiors.

It shows that the working women in our study did not have very good relations with their superiors, although the relations were not bad and strained.

2. Working Women and Colleagues

The relations between colleagues in office is based on equality. Their relations are relatively primary, face-to-face and close. They must share a certain degree of trust and confidence and posses an attitude of help and cooperation. Although the Indian society is advancing on the path of modernisation, it (Indian society) continues to be traditional in terms of occupation, education, and mass media. The social relations between men and women continue to be traditional. For example, men and women workers interact with each other not as individuals in their respective occupational roles, but as men and women. In the following pages, we have tried to analyse the relations of Working Women with their colleagues in office. Our assumption is that their interaction is characterised by social distance.

TABLE VII.5

In Your Opinion, What is the Attitude of (Men) Colleagues Towards Working Women in Office?

Attitude	*To Great Extent*	*To some Extent*	*Never*	*Total*
1. Co-operative and helpful	20 (70)	65 (227)	53 (53)	100 (350)
2. Indifferent and non co-operative	40 (140)	35 (122)	25 (88)	100 (350)
3. Uncooperative	50 (175)	40 (140)	10 (35)	100 (350)

X^2=104. 77, d. f. = 4, significant (p>0. 05) (table value=9. 488)

Note: **Figures in parentheses are actual frequencies.**

Cooperative and Helpful

The attitude of the colleagues towards working women,

as seen from Table VII.5, seems to be favourable. For example only 20 per cent of the respondents said that their colleagues were co-operative and helpful to a great extent, while 65 per cent said it was so only to some extent. The interpretations could be that the respondents' colleagues did not have very close interpersonal relations with them (respondents), although a majority maintained good relations. Personal discussion with the respondents yielded the conclusion that working women had just official relations with their men colleagues. A few respondents even said that they could not expect any help in times of difficulty. Men colleagues, according to the respondents, maintained an attitude of "stay away from women lest one may land in difficulties". Only 15 per cent of the respondents reported that their men colleagues were not co-operative and helpful. It could be concluded that the women workers maintained more official than extra-official relations with their colleagues.

Indifferent and Non-Cooperative

The respondents were asked to react to the question whether or not their colleagues were indifferent and non-cooperative. For example, 40 per cent of the respondents said that their colleagues were indifferent and non-co-operative to a great extent. In other words, they just did not bother about the needs and problems of working women. The respondents reported that men were more interested in their own work. A lady clerk narrated this incident: "I was suffering from fever. I requested a male colleague on phone to inform the office to mark me as on casual leave. But he did not inform the boss. " Some working women reported that men did not want to oblige women colleagues. Men colleagues resented working women's increasing power and authority in office. Many teachers and clerks said men in school / office did not oblige them whenever there were exigencies. A working wife said this: "I was waiting for the suburban bus. But due to rush of passengers, I could not board any bus. A male colleague was passing by, I waved him to stop and requested a lift. He politely refused, perhaps, for fear of public criticisms". But 35 per cent of the respondents said that the indifference and non-cooperativeness was to some extent. It means they experienced indifference and uncooperativeness from men colleagues occasionally. But in the case of 25 per cent of the respondents, there was no question of indifference and non-cooperation on the part of male colleagues. They reported that they were sociable with all staff members. According to this section, most working women were not "social". Therefore, they could not receive positive help from their male workers.

Noncooperative

Respondents were asked to tell whether or not their colleagues were noncooperative in their relationship with working women. A majority (50%) of the respondents felt that male colleagues were highly noncooperative on many occasions. It was reported that men and women interacted not as individuals but as sex beings. Similarly, 40 per cent of the respondents felt that their colleagues were uncooperative to some extent. The data clearly show that, by and large, working women received not much cooperation and help from their colleagues.

To conclude, a maximum of 60 per cent of the working women received cooperation and help to some extent. But a majority of respondents felt their colleagues were indifferent and non-cooperative. Similarly, a majority also felt men colleagues uncooperative.

3. Working Women and Lower Staff

The relationship between working women and the lower staff is characterised by superordination and subordination. Working women may be principals, headmistresses, office managers, section heads; lower staff may consist of lecturers, teachers, clerks, peons etc. As far as power and authority are concerned, working women may be divided in two categories:

1. Women with power and authority such as principals, office managers etc; and
2. Women without power and authority such as lecturers, teachers' clerks, typists etc;

Women who wield power and authority will receive co-operation and help easily, whereas those who do not, may not get the same response. In our sample, about 30 per cent (105) of the respondents were working in administrative and supervisory positions like first and second division clerks, accountants etc. But we have not attempted any analysis according to positions.

TABLE VII.6

In Your Opinion, How Do Lower Men Staff React Towards Working Women?

Attitude	*To Great Extent*	*To some Extent*	*Never*	*Total*
1. Cooperative and helpful	50 (175)	28 (98)	22 (77)	100 (350)
2. Indifferent and non-cooperative	30 (105)	20 (70)	50 (175)	100 (350)
3. Uncooperative	10 (35)	20 (70)	70 (245)	100 (350)

X^2=186. 81, d. f. = 4, significant (p>0. 05) (X^2 >table value=9. 488)
Note: Figures in parentheses are actual frequencies.

1. Cooperation and Help

A bird's eye-view of the data presented in Table VII.6 shows that on the whole the working women in our sample seem to have received co-operation and help from lower staff members. To substantiate, as high as 50 per cent of the respondents said that they were given co-operation and help to a great extent. But a large proportion of those working women who did not occupy any administrative position said that their demands, requests were not met with easily. In order to get their work done, they had to make repeated requests to lower men staff who generally grumbled about obey the working women. But the same staff were very quick and prompt in carrying out orders from those in power and position. A further analysis of the data showed that 28 per cent of the respondents said they got co-operation and help from the lower staff to some extent. But 22 per cent said that they never received any co-operation and help from the lower staff. They were dissatisfied a lot. They had a poor image of the entire organization. In conclusion it may be said that on the whole, working women did not receive much cooperation and help from the lower staff. But those who had power and authority were obeyed by the lower staff.

2. *Indifference and Non-Cooperation*

It appears that the working women in our sample were divided in their responses. For example, 30 per cent and 20 per cent said that the lower staff were indifferent and non-cooperative to a "great extent", and to "some extent" respectively. But 50 per cent of the respondents said the lower staffs were never indifferent and non-cooperative. It is quite possible that this section of the respondents had the skills of managing lower staff members. It means, for the majority, the lower staff did not pose any problem of insubordination.

3. *Noncooperation*

The working women in our sample did not face problems of disobedience, carelessness and negligence on the part of the lower staff, as was indicated by 70 per cent of the respondents. A small proportion (10%) however, experienced non-cooperation on the part of lower staff to a great extent. Similarly, 20 per cent reported that the lower staff did not cooperate with them to some extent. To sum up; the working women in our sample were by and large given cooperation and help by the lower staff. From the above discussion the following conclusions may be drawn:

1. Working women in our sample did not have a good rapport with their male superiors.
2. Relations with the colleagues were not happy.
3. But the working women had relatively good relations with the lower staff.

Working Women and Office Related Functions

At the outset it may be useful and fruitful to point out that a working woman's status not only depends on her performance of duties in office, but also on how she involves herself and takes active part in office related programmes, activities and functions such as marriages, anniversaries, birthdays, picnics etc, Participation in such functions strengthen interpersonal relations among the staff members and thereby boost one's image in peer group circles. In this following paragraphs it is being attempted to analyse how often do working women take active part in social functions?

TABLE VII.7

In Your Opinion, How Often Do Working Women Take Active Part in Office Related Functions?

Programmes	*Very often*	*Often*	*Rarely*	*Total*
1. Get togethers, picnics	25 (87)	20 (70)	55 (193)	100 (350)
2. Farewells, annual gatherings	28 (98)	24 (84)	48 (168)	100 (350)
3. Birthdays, marriage, anniver saries, poojas	48 (168)	22 (77)	30 (106)	100 (350)

X^2=59. 44, d. f. = 4, significant (p>0. 05) (X^2 >table value=9. 488)

Note: Figures in parentheses are actual frequencies.

An overall observation of Table VII.7 gives an impression

that working women's participation in office related social functions is very minimum.

1. Get Together, Picnics

Get-togethers, picnics, tours etc., are arranged by staff members working in any organization. Such programmes constitute an integral part of the informal culture of the organization. Although, participation in such functions is not officially compulsory, but only obligatory, such participation builds and reinforces one's primary relations.

Participation of working women in get-togethers and picnics organized by office staff is not much as a maximum of 25 per cent took active part very often while 20 per cent often enough, and 55 per cent rarely. A majority of the working women, especially married with children, reported that because of family responsibilities, it was very difficult to spare time and participate in programmes. A few, indeed, expressed a strong desire to involve themselves in such functions. But expressed their inability and helplessness.

2. Farewells, Annual Gathering etc.

Participation of working women in programmes like farewells, annual gatherings etc was also not much, For example, 48 per cent of the respondents rarely attended farewells arranged on the occasion of staff members' retirement, transfer or promotion etc. But 28 per cent and 24 per cent of them did attend such functions very often and often respectively. It means 52 per cent of them attended such functions. According to them, it was important for them to attend farewells arranged in honour of their colleagues and annual gatherings, which are equally important as office duties.

3. Birthdays, Marriage Ceremonies, Anniversaries

Birthdays, marriages, and marries anniversaries of staff members are not directly related to office. But attending such programmes of staff members becomes important since such staff happen to be their colleagues in office whose co-operation is essential and inevitable to conduct office work. As high as 48 per cent of the respondents attended birthdays, marriage ceremonies, anniversaries very often, while 22 per cent often. This could be interpreted as that a majority of the working women, under investigation, generally took interest in attending social functions. According to the respondents attending marriage ceremonies, anniversaries, poojas etc was not only important from the social point of view, but also from religious and spiritual points of view. But those who rarely attended such functions gave reasons which were very routine and usual viz-family difficulties, pregnancy, etc. One thing that can be discerned from the data is that the proportion of respondents who attended marriage ceremonies etc was larger than that of those who attended get-togethers or farewells etc. From the analysis of the above data the following conclusions may be reached.

1. Working women could not evince much interest in social functions such as get-togethers, picnics etc arranged by staff members.
2. Similarly, working women could not attend functions like farewells etc.
3. However, a greater proportion of them attended and took active part in social functions like marriage ceremonies, birthday anniversaries of their colleagues, superiors and menial staff members.

Working Women and Union Activities

Workers unions / associations are an integral part of any organization. They function as a link between the workers and the management. Their main objective is to protect and guard the workers against highhandedness and exploitation by the management and or the govt. A union is an organization of wage-earners to protect and promote the interests of wage-earners and to enable them to contribute according to their ability and experience to social and industrial enterprise.

Unions may be viewed as voluntary organisations of workers or employees formed to promote and protect their interests through collective action. According to Serlekar (1986: 416) , a union is an organisation of employees to play the role of a collective bargaining agent for its own members, negotiate wages, hours of work, bonuses, working conditions, terms and conditions of service and such other vital problems affecting the employees directly. It is a powerful instrument to promote and safeguard the interest of workers and to achieve the economic, psychological, and social goals of workers.

Union activities involve a lot of politicking, lobbying, pressurizing and underhand dealings. In the following pages it is intended to know the part played by working women in union activities. We have taken into account the following factors for analysis.

1. Membership of union.
2. Reasons for becoming or not becoming a member, and
3. Participation in protest programmes.

1. Membership of Union

Membership of the union is an integral part of the working woman's social status. Membership of the union provides rights, security and responsibilities. It enables the working woman to enter a new world of union members. Unions are instruments of collective bargaining. Thus membership of the union is an important determinant of the working woman's social status.

TABLE VII.8

Are You a Member of the Staff Union?

Response	*Fr*	%
Yes	185	53
No	165	47
	350	100

A majority (53%) of the respondents were members of the union, while 47 per cent were not. It means, roughly, half of the sample did not register itself as members of the union.

Reasons for Becoming Member

The respondents who were members of the staff union were asked to specify reasons, which are presented in the table below.

TABLE VII.9

If Yes, What are Your Reasons?

Reasons	*Fr*	%
1. Pressure of Friends	74	40
2. Helps in redressing injustice	70	38
3. Unity and organization	41	22
	185	100

A study of the reasons given by the respondents for becoming union members indicates lack of articulation and direction. For example, 40 per cent were members because their friends forced them. This indicates, such members primarily were not attracted by the union. Their membership was nominal. Such members do not contribute towards strengthening and developing the union. They are as good as no members. But significantly 38 per cent of the members said that they became members because the union helped them in redressing their grievances or injustice. Similarly, 22 per cent stressed that the union provides unity and organization. On the whole, 60 per cent of those who were union members believed in the advantages of the union.

Reasons for Not Becoming Members

We have seen that 53 per cent of the respondents were members of the union. Obviously, 47 per cent of them were not members. When asked why they did not become members, the following reasons were given.

TABLE VII.10

What are Your Reasons for Not Becoming Member?

Reasons	*Fr*	%
1. I am a junior	33	20
2. Unions do not serve any purpose	82	50
3. Not interested	50	30
	165	100

A look at Table VII.10 shows that half of the respondents who were not members of the union did not believe in the efficacy and usefulness of the union in serving the needs of the members. When asked to elaborate further, they said unions are centers of politics and vested interests. Its leaders serve their own interests more than the interests of the members. They just did not believe in the union. Another 30 percent of the respondents said that they were not interested in the union due to personal and family reasons.

To sum up: Roughly half of the working women in the sample were members of the union. Of the half (165), 60 per cent (111) believed in the efficacy and usefulness of the union. Of the remaining 47 per cent, a majority did not believe in the union as an organization of workers. Thirty (30%) per cent of them said that they were not interested in becoming members of the union. It could be concluded that working women were not very much interested in unions. This will isolate them from the larger activities of the union.

Participation of Working Women in Union Activities

In this section we would like to know the participation of the working women in the sample in union activities. Participation of the working women in union activities will not only expose them to collective bargaining, but also integrate them with the larger work force. It also indicates their courage, determination, and will power to fight against injustice and exploitation. Effective functioning of democracy depends upon people's willingness to fight against injustice and desire to sacrifice for the common cause.

TABLE VII.11

In Your Opinion, How Often Do Working Women Take Active Part in Union Activities to Protest against Injustice by the Management/Govt.?

Union Activities	*Very often*	*Often*	*Rarely*	*Total*
1. Protests, submission of memos	26 (91)	30 (105)	44 (154)	100 (350)
2. Strikes, bundhs	10 (35)	22 (77)	68 (238)	100 (350)
3. Hunger strikes	10 (35)	15 (52)	75 (263)	100 (350)

X^2=80. 61, d. f. = 4 significant (p>0. 05) (table value=9. 488)
Note: Figures in parentheses are actual frequencies.

Information was gathered from working women was gathered about three types of union activities to protest against injustice by the management /Govt.

1. Protests, submission of memos
2. Strikes,Bandhs, Processions
3. Hunger strikes.

1. Protests, Submission of Memos

Protests, submission of memos is a form of resolving differences of opinion between groups. This may be considered the first step of democratic procedure. The aggrieved party submits a memorandum of disagreement and resentment towards a policy, notification etc. According to the respondents' reactions, only 26 per cent participated very often, while 30 per cent said 'often'. It means 56 percent of the respondents took part in protests in varying degrees. They said participation of working women in protests is important. They said their responsibility is as great as that of men. But 44 per cent of the respondents rarely took part in protest programmes. Some pleaded family responsibilities, while others said that participation in protest programmes may lead to retaliation from the management. They are prepared to tolerate injustice rather than incur the wrath of the management, they said. Nevertheless, the working women's response in this regard was favourable.

2. Strikes, Bandhs, Processions

Strikes, bandhs, processions are relatively action oriented forms of protest. They involve physical and mental actions. Compared to the first category of protest viz, submission of memos, press statements and such, the second category of protest involves risk, danger, manhandling, clash with police etc. Such actions invite public wrath and management's displeasure. Under such circumstances, more women than men are likely to keep themselves away from involvement. A look at the data reveals that an overwhelming majority of the sample did not take active part in strikes, bandhs, and processions. It shows their unwillingness and lack of interest in union activities. The respondents gave two reasons:

1. Their parents / parents-in-law / husbands do not allow them to participate in such union activities, as it will endanger their family prestige, and

2. The Govt. or management may nurse a grudge against such womei., and may victimize them later.

Uma Ramswamy (1992: 100), in her article "Women and Work", discusses the interaction between women workers and trade unions. According to her, women workers admit that their husbands discourage and even prohibit them from getting embroiled in union affairs. Husbands do not want their women folk to go beyond mere payment of membership fee and limited involvement when they (women) themselves are likely to face problems at work. They (husbands/parents) do not want their wives or daughters to be union activists. Taking up union activity, in their view, involved contact with a mixed crowd. It was best that women avoided coming under the public gaze.

However, it is significant to observe that 10 per cent and 22 per cent of the respondents did take part in strikes, bandhs and processions very often and often, respectively. In other words, 32 per cent of the respondents participated in risk-involving union activities. They advocated that union activities are part of organizations. Women, like men, should equally involve themselves in union activities, and they (women) need not entertain apprehensions. From the above discussion, it can be stated that a majority of the women workers, in our study, were not interested in risk-based union activities.

3. Hunger Strikes

Hunger strikes are adopted by unions as the last democratic resort to get grievances redressed. Only a few selected individuals can go on hunger strike. This method is adopted in order to attract and mobilise public opinion. The respondents' reactions to hunger strikes seemed to be very lukewarm and negative. As high a proportion as 75 per cent of the respondents very rarely took part in hunger strikes, while only ten per cent and 15 per cent took part in hunger strikes very often, and often, respectively. It means around 25 per cent of the respondents reacted positively to hunger strikes called by the unions to protest against actions of the Govt. or management. It follows from the above discussion that working women rarely evinced more than a passing interest in union activities.

SUMMARY

This chapter intends to analyse the status and role of the working woman in office or at the work place. There are differences of opinion among researchers about the status and role of the working woman in office. Studies by Ramanamma (1979), Lalithadevi (1982) and others have shown that working women enjoy a higher status in office. On the other hand, studies by sociologists like Bhoite (1987) have concluded that working women do not enjoy a higher status. We have tried to explore the changing status of the working woman in office. Our assumption is that since the Indian society has not changed significantly, the working woman is likely to face many problems of adjustment in office. The status and role of the working woman are studied, taking into account the following factors.

1. Working women and interpersonal relations with men and women colleagues,
2. Working women and efficiency,
3. Attitudes of male workers towards female workers as perceived by the latter,
4. Attitudes of higher officers, colleagues, and lower staff towards working women
5. Working women's active participation in office functions, and
6. Working women and union activities.

1. Our data have revealed that working women maintained more friendly and harmonious relations with women than men.
2. Working women felt that they could not perform their duties in office satisfactorily due to family responsibilities.
3. The study had revealed that the respondents felt that male workers had a poor conceptual image of working women. The respondents felt that they could not be very punctual, efficient, sociable and hard working due to family responsibilities.
4. Higher officers had a negative attitude towards working women. The relations between working women and their colleagues were not very happy. But the relations between working women and the lower staff were cordial.
5. Working women could not take an active part in social functions. Very few respondents attended marriages, birthday anniversaries of their colleagues.
6. Most working women were not members of the union. In fact most did not believe it is a useful organisation. Very few respondents participated in union activities.

In conclusion it may be said that working women in our sample were not fully integrated with office culture.

8

Summary and Conclusion

INTRODUCTION

The concept of working woman in India is a recent phenomenon. This, however, does not mean that women did not engage themselves in work outside the home. Women worked for wages in farms and fields in rural areas, in towns and cities women worked in the construction sector etc. But women's participation in economic activities was limited to agriculture, construction etc. Generally, women from the poorer sections, backward and lower classes, engaged in a kind of work participation. Work outside the home was not secured.

In modern times, thè phrase 'working woman' connotes a different meaning. It means working in offices, schools, hospitals etc. The advent of industrialisation urbanisation and modern education in the last five decades has given rise to a variety of modern jobs, occupations and professions, which involve more formal education. Modern occupations are relatively secular, non-manual and menial and free from gender biases.

Besides, the advent of Independence of India and acceptance of a new constitution by India has created a favourable situation, especially in urban areas, to take to modern education and employment. Obviously, the emerging phenomenon of 'Working Woman' in modern India has deeper and wider implications for the women themselves, for the family and the society at large. As Desai and Anantharam (1985) observe;" middle class women's outside work participation is not merely an economic activity but it affects norms regarding the proper sphere of women, their status vis-à-vis their husbands, values underlying patriarchal family structure, redefinition of the roles of family members, care of children, mixing with other men and remaining outside the house for long hours".

1. Differences of Opinion

There are equally sharp differences of opinion about the changes taking place in the position of women in India. Some regard these changes as profound and pervasive; they point to the increasing participation of women in public life and to the changes introduced in their legal status (Kapur, 1974; Mishra, 1993; Lalitha devi, 1982). Others maintain that the position of Women has changed very little and that Indian society continues, by and large, to be a male-dominated society (Beteille, 1975: 61).

It follows that the part played by employment of woman in raising her status and role is not yet well documented. Therefore, there is a need for further research into the subject. The following research questions are being asked in this regard:

- Does employment of woman bring about a greater degree of change towards the equality of status for woman in a society which continues to be traditional and stratified in its social set up?
- What happens to the role and status of educated women when they are employed, in the context of a traditional society like the Indian?
- Does employment act as an agent of modernisation in bringing about attitudinal changes in educated

working women towards traditional social issues such as women's education and employment, and marriage and family, or does it not?

- Why do educated women take to employment?
- Is or is not employment sought as a means of earning money or a career?
- How do educated working women perceive the importance of education and employment vis-a-vis their traditional role and status?
- Are working women becoming modern in their attitudes towards marriage as a sacrament; mate selection; love marriage; dowry; widow marriage etc? If yes, to what extent?
- Are working women becoming modern in their outlook towards joint or nuclear family?
- Do working women tend to establish a nuclear family or a mix of both?
- Do working women perceive any change in their position in relation to husband, parents-in-law?
- Are working women involved in decision-making in the family? If so, to what extent?
- Do family members share domestic chores? If so, to what extent?
- How do working women interact with their office colleagues?
- Do working women participate in social functions of their colleagues?
- Do working women evince interest in union activities?

Hypothesis

The present study intends to test the hypothesis that employment of woman brings about significant changes in terms of equality of status and her role vis-a-vis family and office. Our assumption is that since the Indian society continues to be relatively conservative, rigid, backward and stratified, changes in the economic role of the woman are not likely to bring about worthwhile changes.

Objectives of the Study

The chief objective of the study is to analyse the influence of employment on the role and status of the educated woman.

Specific Objectives of the Study

The specific objectives of the study are:

II. To study if working women were becoming modern towards social issues viz women's education , employment and marriage and family.

1. *Education:*

   To study the attitudes of working women towards:

   (a) Aims of higher education in relation to women,

   (b) Levels of education for women,

   (c) Working women as better wives, better mothers, makers and managers of home.

2. *Employment:*

   To study the attitudes of working women towards:

   (a) Reasons for taking up employment

   (b) Sources of motivation for employment,

   (c) Continuing in job after marriage

   (d) Career versus marriage

3. *Marriage:*

   To find out whether there is any change in the attitudes of working women with regard to:

(a) Divorce
(b) Mate choice
(c) Love marriage versus arranged marriage
(d) Dowry
(e) Widow re-marriage
(f) Family planning

3. *Family:*

To examine the changing views of working women about

(a) Reasons for staying in the joint family
(b) Reasons for opting for a nuclear family
(c) Interaction between joint and nuclear families

II. To find out the changing status and role of working women in relation to family members:

(a) To analyse the position as perceived by the respondents in relation to husband and parents-in-law
(b) To know if the working women have any freedom to buy
(c) To whether or not the working women are involved in decision making regarding family matters
(d) To find out if other family members shared the domestic chores of the family and
(f) To analyse whether the working women faced any problems of adjustment with the husband and parents-in-law

III. To study if the working women are accorded their due status and role in office; more specifically, it was intended

(a) To find out about the interpersonal relations (trust and confidence) with men and women colleagues,

(b) To ascertain how the working women perceived their efficiency in office in relation to men

(c) To know the attitude of the male workers – co-operative, or non-cooperative or uncooperative towards female workers.

(d) To study the attitudes of the office staff – superiors, colleagues and subordinates towards working women,

(e) To analyse if the working women took active part in office functions; and,

(f) To understand the attitudes of working women towards workers unions with regard to membership and participation in union activities like submission of memorandums, taking out processions and going on hunger strikes.

1. Need for the Present Study

A survey of the literature available on working women revealed that very few studies have focused their attention on 1) educated (graduate) working women; and 2) such, with confirmed jobs in the organised sector. Taking the above factors into account the present study was undertaken.

2. Theoretical Framework

The theoretical perspective used in the study is Tradition and Modernity. To be specific, modernisation in terms of scientific temper, rationalisation, equality, secularism, can bring about changes within the fundamentals of a tradition. For example, a woman in India cannot claim equality or superiority with the husband, parents and parents-in-law, however well educated and employed she may be. Any significant deviation from the fundamentals of tradition will lead to a crisis of values. A working wife can enjoy higher status only when she plays a balanced role of wife in the family and employee in the office. Modernisation requires simultaneous changes in the working women, her family members and office staff.

3. Status and Role: A Conceptual Analysis

1. Status

Generally, the term "status" is understood as rights, power/ authority and privileges. But the meaning of status is relative to the status-set with whom the incumbent is related as husband and wife etc. Therefore, in reality the meaning of status has to be understood in terms of status-set.

2. Role

The term 'role' refers to one's duties, responsibilities. Like the term status, the role should also be comprehended in terms of role-sets. Role and status always go together.

3. Status of Woman

The status of woman has to be defined, taking account of her socio-economic and physical-biological disabilities. It further varies according to the ideological and religious values of a given society. According to Malinowski (1949), a correct definition of status of Woman can be given only after taking into consideration all mutual duties between the sexes, and the safeguards provided for the protection of each sex against the high-handedness of the other. Lowie (1913) has shown that status may mean four different things, all the four of which may not, however, be found to exist together anywhere. Thus, actual treatment, legal status, opportunities for social participation and the character and extent of work all taken together determine, each in a specific sense and manner, the status of woman in a society. Mukherjee (1975) has proposed a comprehensive definition of status of woman. 'Status of women' refers to a set of expectations regarding the attributes pertaining to the duties and responsibilities of women in their roles as daughter, wife, mother, worker, and member of the household etc, and the actions, rewards or rights which they expect from others' in these positions as well as others perception of the actual rewards accompanying these positions (29).

4. Universes and Methodology

The study was conducted in Gulbarga city of Karnataka. Graduate women, working in various offices, educational institutions, banks located in Gulbarga city constituted the respondents. A census of women workers with graduation as minimum level of education was conduced. Out of 1,600 working women with confirmed service finally 350 respondents were selected by using the stratified sampling method.

5. Socio-economic Profile of the Respondents

1. The Working Women's Background

The socio-economic profile of the respondents, under investigation, revealed the diverse composition of the sample. A majority of the respondents were young (41%) and adults (44%). Hindus were found in majority (67%). Roughly, half of the respondents were post-graduates (47%), while the remaining (53%) were graduates. A majority (70%) of the respondents were from urban background and were married (75%). Occupationally, the respondents were distributed into low jobs (42%) like clerks, teachers; medium jobs (25%) like supervisors, administrators; and higher jobs (30%) like doctors, engineers etc.

2. Husbands' Background

A majority (83%) of the husbands of the respondents had college and university education. Seventy-eight (78%)

per cent of the husbands were engaged in white-collar jobs, while 22 per cent were traders and businessmen.

3. Parents' Background

A majority of the fathers had studied from S. S. L. C. (32%) up to post graduation (40%) and SSLC (32%). But 28 per cent were illiterate. Data on mother's education indicated that 40 per cent of the mothers had education between 7th and 10th standard. Occupationally, 58 per cent of the fathers were engaged in white-collar jobs, while 22 per cent were in business. The remaining 20 per cent were agriculturist. A majority (78%) of the mothers were housewives, while 22 per cent were employed in low and medium jobs. It could be concluded that parents' educational and occupational background was relatively encouraging.

4. Parents-in-law's Background

The educational background of the parents-in-law was not very high. Information gathered about the father-in-laws' education indicated that 50 per cent had studied up to primary school. But 30 per cent of them had studied up to 7th standard, while a 20 per cent segment included PUC pass and undergraduates.

The educational background of the mothers-in-law was very poor. Fifty-eight (58%) per cent of them were illiterates. About 30 per cent of the fathers-in law had education up to the 7th standard. Only 12 per cent had completed SSLC. The occupational background of the parents-in-law was equally low. For example, 46 per cent of them were engaged in white-collar jobs, 22 per cent were pursuing agriculture. Data on mother-in-laws' occupation revealed that 70 per cent were housewives, while a maximum of 30 per cent were working in white-collar jobs like school teachers, clerks, peons. It follows that both the parents-in-law had ordinary educational and occupational background. From the above analysis of the social background of the respondents the following conclusions may be drawn:

1. A majority of the respondents were highly educated.
2. A majority of the respondents were young and adults.
3. A majority (67%) of the respondents were Hindus, while Christians (12%) and Muslims (20%) constituted about 33 per cent.
4. A majority of the respondents were married and came from an urban background.
5. Most respondents were engaged in low and medium jobs.
6. A majority of the husbands were relatively well educated and employed in white-collar jobs. In conclusion it may be said that, relatively speaking, the respondents and their husbands came from an elite background.
7. Among the respondents' parents, a majority of the fathers were well educated and engaged in white-collar jobs. But most mothers were illiterate and housewives.
8. A majority of the fathers-in-law were poorly educated and engaged in agriculture and business. Similarly, a majority of the mothers-in-law were illiterates and housewives.

Modernisation of Working Women

Working women's attitudes, values and outlooks will play a significant part in enabling them to adjust with the emerging problems of home and office in consequence of employment. To be more specific, modernisation involves the question whether the working women are relatively rational, liberal, secular, egalitarian and pragmatic in their attitudes and values towards traditional and modern ways of life. For example, what are the attitudes of the working women towards women's education and employment, marriage and family. The definition of the role and status of the working women depends to the extent they, relatively, have become modernised. For example, how do working women view the importance of education in general and higher education in particular in relation to traditional roles of wife and mother?

With the acceptance of democracy based on liberty, equality and fraternity, special emphasis is being laid on the development of the weaker sections, including women by providing opportunities for education and employment. Women are supposed to receive education and seek employment and work alongside of men and thereby contribute their mite towards national reconstruction. Scholars like Inkles (1969) and Anderson and Shills (1966), who have done extensive research in the field of education, have shown that rapid change in social values and existing norms of a developing country can take place only when there is spread of female education. Female education is supposed to provide employment opportunities and make women enlightened wives, mothers, and managers of home. In the following pages, it is intended to analyse.

1. Attitudes towards Aims of Higher Education in Relation to Women.
2. Levels of Education.
3. Working woman as a better wife, mother, and manager of home and as a social being.
4. Attitude towards employment:
   (1) Reasons for taking up employment
   (2) Sources of motivation for employment
   (3) Continuing in job after marriage
   (4) Employment versus marriage

5. Attitudes towards marriage and family
   (1) Marriage as a sacrament
   (2) Divorce
   (3) Mate selection
   (4) Love marriage versus arranged marriage
   (5) Dowry, widow re-marriage, family planning, and
   (6) Changing status of joint family.

Let us analyse the subject.

ATTITUDE TOWARDS AIMS OF HIGHER EDUCATION IN RELATIONS TO WOMEN

It is important to know whether or not working women had positive attitudes towards women having higher education. Favourable attitude towards women having higher education indicates their outlook for the changing status of women. Our aim was to know how the working women perceived the aims of higher education. Generally, higher education for women was believed to be mere acquisition of a degree. But higher education in modern India has come to be entrenched into all walks of life. Answering the question as to what were the aims of higher education with regard to women, 70 per cent of the sample expressed the view that higher education was supposed to make them (women) fit for modern life. Thereby they meant that education should help them in combining the old and new values of life. Twenty (20%) per cent, and 10 per cent, said that education was supposed to enable them play a woman's traditional role of wife better, and seek employment, respectively. It could be concluded that working women felt that higher education would help them in adapting to the challenges of modernisation.

Level of Education for Women

Generally, women were not encouraged to receive higher education in the past. But the importance of education is being realised by educated men and women nowadays. The respondents were being asked as to how much education should women be given. A maximum of 50 per cent wanted women to have college and university education, while 40 per cent recommended SSLC as the maximum. On the whole, working women favoured women having higher levels of education.

The findings of Kumud Ranjan (1993), Pratima Kumari (1988), Sethi (1976), Kaur (1983), have indicated similar responses from working women towards women's education.

Education and Women's Traditional Role

Education in modern society has come to play a significant role in transforming the traditional society. Respondents were asked to indicate the role of education in transforming the traditional roles of women as wife, mother, manager of home and social individual. A majority of the respondents gave a positive reply, stating that education equipped them with knowledge, awareness and skills so as to adapt them to the changing needs of modern life. Thus, it could be concluded that education with regard to women has come to be regarded as an asset.

Working Women and Employment

The role and status of the working woman depends upon whether employment is taken up as a career option or a temporary measure. Our aim was to find out how strongly the working women were motivated to take up employment. Our assumption was that those who want to stand on their feet, are self motivated and are determined to be in jobs even after marriage, are likely to resolve the problems of home and office successfully. In the present study the following factors were considered.

1. Reasons for taking up employment
2. Sources of motivation for employment
3. Desire to continue in job even after marriage, and
4. Attitude towards employment versus marriage

1. Reasons for Taking Up Employment

The main reasons advanced by the respondents were rooted in a desire to achieve independent status. For example, 50 per cent wanted to support themselves, while 26 per cent and 24 per cent were interested in raising the standard of the family and securing economic independence. The data clearly showed that the working women were mainly interested in improving the class status of the family and thereby acquire a well-defined individual status in society. To quote Kapur (1978), "Educated women are gradually realising that work is not a necessary evil, but a way of living a full life and provides a possibility for self-realisation. It may be concluded that the working women, under investigation, were interested in raising their social status.

2. Sources of Motivation

Analysis of data on the sources of motivation revealed that it was parents / parents-in-law (50%) who mainly acted as the source of motivation women for taking up employment. However, 40 per cent of the respondents made self-efforts by browsing through newspapers, gazette notices etc. It may be stated that choice of employment was the result of pressures jointly felt by respondents themselves and the family members.

3. Desire to Continue in Job Even after Marriage

It is generally believed that educated women take up employment as a stop-gap-arrangement until they are married. But the situation in modern times has changed in view of the emerging socio-economic pressures. Educated women are placing a greater premium on employment than on marriage. When asked: Should working women continue in their jobs after marriage? an overwhelming majority (88%) gave a positive reply. They said marriage and family do not become a hindrance to continuing in a job.

4. Employment Verses Marriage

To make sure of the employed women's determination to continue in their jobs, one more attempt was made. It was intended to know what employed women would do if they were forced to make a choice between employment and marriage? As high as 68 per cent did not agree with the proposition. They said marriage and employment cannot be put against each other. Both are integral part of modern life, they added. However, 20 per cent preferred marriage and give up job, while 12 per cent wanted employment and do away with marriage. But the majority did not anticipate such situations in life.

To sum up, our respondents were strongly motivated for employment. Both parents and respondents were equally interested in seeking employment. According to most working women employment did not pose any threat to marital relations.

Marriage as a Sacrament

Marriage among the Hindus is a sacrament, the solemnization of a holy union of two souls. As a sacrament, it is supposed to purify the human body, soul and mind and qualify for Moksha attainment of divine-hood. The philosophy of Hindu marriage does not make provision for divorce, especially for women. Divorce among Hindus is considered a sin.

Traditionally both husband and wife were prohibited from seeking divorce, because, by and large, Hindu philosophy does not believe in divorce. The philosophy of Hindu marriage, again, fundamentally believes in the inherent inequality of men and women. The respondents were asked to indicate their attitudes towards divorce. It is important to observe that 80 per cent of the respondents disagreed with the statement that marriage among Hindus was a holy union of two souls and divorce could not be granted under any conditions. It clearly indicates that our sample of working women did not accept marriage as a sacrament. Their disagreement with the statements revealed a change of views. Their disagreement gave the clue that divorce could be granted or sought under exceptional conditions. In the same line another question was asked. Under what conditions should divorce be allowed for husband and wife? As high as 60 per cent of the respondents expressed the view that divorce could be allowed to husband and wife under extreme conditions of maladjustment and unbearable said that divorce could be given to a wife, if her husband married a second wife. It becomes clear that the working women, under investigation, are no longer prepared to accept the sacramental character of Hindu marriage. A change in their mood is clearly visible. This does not, however, mean that there is a radical change in the attitudes of working women towards marriage as a sacrament. Further discussion with the respondents revealed that they did not believe in the sacramental character of marriage. What they said was that they accept marriage as a sacrament. But if the relations between husband and wife become unbearable, control, divorce should be granted.

Mate Selection: Choice of Life Partner

According to Robert Blood (1967) as the rigid system of stratification becomes flexible, the "familistic" mate selection pattern is replaced by the self-mate selection pattern. Thus the replacement of the rigid stratification system in Hindu society by the flexible type may lead to freedom for the youngsters in the selection of their life partners. In the traditional Indian society parents and Kin-people played a major role in deciding the marriage of sons and daughters. Fixing and arranging the marriage of youths was the prerogative of the parents, and kinsmen. But slowly traditional values and practices associated with mate selection are undergoing a change.

Industrialisation, urbanization, modern education and mass media have played a significant role in developing independent thinking in human beings, especially among youths. In this regard, it is important to know the attitudes of working women towards mate selection. To be more specific, it was attempted to find out whether or not, the working women were prepared to grant freedom to their children with regard to mate selection. The respondents were also asked to indicate as to who should take the decision. The respondents were given three options: 1) Parents 2) Parents with self, and 3) self-choice. As high as 58 per cent said that mate selection cannot be left to the boy or the girl, as marriage is a family affair. It should be decided by both parents and wards. It is a joint venture, they said. However, 33 per cent were in favour of self-choice. Such respondents argued that wards should be given full freedom to decide about their life partner and be made responsible for their actions. But hardly 9 per cent wanted parents to decide everything. It follows that a significant change is taking place in the minds of working women towards modernization. They are recognizing the emerging phenomenon of modern youth.

Love Marriage/Arranged Marriage

There is a growing feeling among researchers that with modernization educated working women tend to prefer love marriage to arranged marriage (Giriraj Khanna 1978; Kapur, 1970; Giriraj Gupta, 1976). The assumption, however, was not based on any extensive and indepth research. It was felt that such radical departures in Indian society are not likely to occur. Respondents were asked: if women were given full freedom to marry, what form of marriage (love marriage or arranged marriage) would they adopt? As high as 50 per cent did not believe in any extreme form of marriage viz arranged or love marriage. Interestingly they basically believed in arranged marriage but with freedom of choice. But 30 per cent of the respondents still stuck to arranged marriage regardless of the ward's interests and tastes. Similarly, 20 per cent believed in love marriage regardless of elders' likes and dislikes. Our finding was that working women believed in arranged marriage but were prepared to accept change so far as giving freedom to wards in choosing their life partners. Our finding is in agreement with earlier studies by Gore (1968) and Kurian, (1974). Prakash Rao and Nandini Rao (1982) too arrived at the same conclusion.

Attitudes Towards Dowry

The practice of dowry is an indication of women's low status. Ideally, there could be enhancement in the status of women, only if the practice is abolished. Indeed, according to law, the practice of dowry does stand abolished. But in reality the practice of dowry has become much stronger than in the past. Modernisation has not succeeded in abolishing dowry. Most of our respondents believed in dowry and its functions. Indeed dowry gave them status and security. But, the respondents said that employment provided some relief from dowry. According to the respondents it was almost impossible to abolish dowry. It seems most unlikely that the requirement of dowry will be discontinued with the education and employment of women. The problem of dowry is rooted in the system of arranged marriage and while it may provide the bride with security and facilitate upward social mobility, it also encourages a view of woman as a commodity with a market price that varies according to her education and complexion and the boys' occupation "(Mamdani, 1972).

The study has also shown that employment of woman has not made much difference for payment of dowry. The one change that was observed was that a working woman was relatively easily preferred in marriage with liberal concessions for dowry, sub-caste,family background and complexion of the girl.

Changing Status of Widows

It has been already stated that Hindu marriage, as a sacrament, does not make provision for widow marriage. Widowhood implied a great deal of hardship and suffering. The widow was almost treated like an untouchable in the past, especially among caste Hindus.

Significant changes are taking place in the status of widows. Traditional taboos and prejudices associated with widows are being eroded. Widows at least in urban areas are not despised as much as they used to be. A greater degree of positive change in the attitudes of society towards the windows is visible. Nevertheless, there is no fundamental change in society's attitudes toward the widows. For example, 70 per cent favoured widow remarriage. According to the respondents widow remarriage was not wrong. It provided an opportunity for a new life and equal right. But the respondents favoured remarriage of working widows who without children. After a deep probe into the inner feelings, it was observed that the working women favoured the idea of remarriage of working widows, whether they had children or not. It appears that employment does make a difference to the status of the working widow.

Planned Parenthood

With the advent of modernization, radical changes have been taking place in the composition and functioning of marriage and family in the world. The philosophy of the small family norm has encompassed the whole world. Our aim was to analyse the attitude of the working women towards small family. It goes without saying that educated working women are favourable towards the small family. It may be useful to examine the adoption of a small family norms, viz., parents and two children, against the background of ideological aims and objectives of marriage and family. For example, in India from religious and spiritual point of view, it is important to have children in general, and male children in particular. Whether a working woman adopts small family norm depends on her having male children. A working woman with two daughters will adopt the small family norm out of sheer frustration and economic compulsion. The present study has revealed that a majority of the respondents believed in family planning and its benefits for the children,, parents and the entire family. A majority (65%) of the respondents wanted to have a maximum of two children, while 25 per cent preferred just one child. But when the respondents were asked to indicate if they were prepared to adopt family planning by undergoing tubectomy operation in case they had only male children, both male and female children and only female children. It is important to note that as high as 60 per cent of the respondents preferred to undergo operation if they had both male and female children. About 30 per cent said that working women should stop bearing children if they had only two male children. Interestingly, personal discussion with the respondents revealed that those who had only daughters were unhappy and hopeless. They felt that there would be no successor to their family. It may be stated that employment has created tensions and fears about children. The working woman is in a dilemma.

Working Women and the Joint Family

It is commonly held that the traditional system of joint family is disintegrating in modern India, paving the way for the emergence of a nuclear form of family. The underlying assumption is that, with the introduction of industrialisation and urbanisation, spread of modern education and mass media, there is a growing tendency to change over from the joint family to a nuclear family. But there are differences of opinion about the changing status of joint family because of lack of agreement about the precise definition of joint family. Our aim was to examine whether or not the working women tended to opt for the nuclear family consisting of husband, wife and their unmarried children. Joint family was understood from three points of view:

1. A group consisting of parents, married sons and their children and unmarried children
2. A group consisting of parents and a married son with other unmarried children, and,
3. A group consisting of husband and wife with their unmarried children along with one or two ego's kins.

The data collected in this regard have shown that out of 350 respondents, 200 or 57 per cent had been living in joint families (I & II types), while 43 per cent had been living in nuclear families (III type). Respondents were clear about the advantages and disadvantages of both forms of families. The 53 per cent of the respondents who lived in joint families did not have any problems of adjustment with the members. It was observed that those who lived in joint families were able to combine the needs of nuclear and joint families.

Another attempt was made to know whether there was any interaction between joint families and nuclear families. It was found that there was harmonious interaction between the two forms of families. According to respondents living in separate nuclear families, they have not severed relationships with their parents / brothers and sisters and other members. It could be even stated that the emergence of the nuclear family has strengthened the foundations of the joint family. In short, the working women, under investigation, believed in the joint family, while acknowledging the importance of the nuclear family. Our data do not support the assumption that working women tend to opt for the nuclear type. The reasons for living in nuclear families were varied viz. lack of space, transfer of job etc. It was also observed that nuclear families were joint families in their functions. It appears that both forms are reinforcing each other. Under such conditions of family change, the working women have to claim their newly acquired status within the framework of the Indian family. Our findings are in agreement with the findings of M.S. Gore (1968), Milton Singer (1968), Prakash Rao and Nandini Rao (1982)

To sum up: The working women in the sample have a favourable and positive attitude towards higher education and employment of women. According to them education will help women become a better wife and mother. It will provide opportunities for employment. It could be said that there is a change in the perception of the working women regarding their status. Modernization in terms of education and employment is well within the boundaries of tradition.

However, the working women were found to be relatively traditional with regard to marriage and family. Employment has not brought about radical changes in their attitudes towards marriage and family. Therefore, change in their status is restricted to their attitudes towards marriage and family.

Status and Role of Working Woman in the Family

The concept of status and role of woman has been defined in terms of rights, power, authority and responsibilities, duties, and obligations. Education and employment have made women aware have made women aware of their rights and given power to assert their individuality. One may ask: Does employment ensure equality of rights, power, authority, and responsibilities in the family?

Studies conducted by Srivastawa, (1978), Indiradevi (1987), Talwar, (1984) have come to the conclusion that there are significant changes in the status and role of the working woman. There are other studies which do not support the finding. For example, Kapur (1973) found that although the working woman was allowed to take part in the decision-making process in the family, her decision was not final. It shows that the hypothesis that employment raises the status of the working woman needs to be further tested. In order to analyse the changing status of the working woman, five dimensions of woman's status were considered.

1. Position as perceived by the respondents in the family.
2. Freedom to act.
3. Involvement in decision-making
4. Problems of adjustment in family.

Blood and Wolfe (1960) have attempted to explain the role of employment in bringing about changes in the status of the working woman by using the Resource Theory of Power. It was intended to analyse whether or not employment enhanced the status of the working woman.

1. Position of Working Woman in the Family

The economic status of a woman has a deep bearing on her social status in the family and society. The working women in the sample were asked to indicate their perception regarding their position in the family in relation to husband, parents-in-law, brothers-in-law and other members. It was found that 40 per cent of them felt their status to be equal with that of their husbands, while 60 per cent said it was lower. Those who equated their status with the status of their husbands said that their husbands treated them as equals and shared their household duties. According to them both lived more like friends than as husband and wife. But the remaining 60 per cent, who believed their status lower than that of their husbands, considered their husbands superior as they were heads of the family. According to them a wife can never be equal to her husband. It was observed in case of these working wives that the educational and occupational statuses of their husbands were higher. It is quite possible that the higher-class status of the husbands might have influenced their (wives) perception.

Data with regard to the perception of working women's position in relation to parents-in-law revealed that 20 per cent of the respondents considered their status higher than that of their parents-in-law, while 40 per cent said 'equal' and the remaining 40 per cent 'low'. In the case of 20 per cent of the respondents who said that their status was higher than that of their parents-in-law, the possible reasons may have been that the parents-in-law were less educated and engaged in lower occupations. Perhaps similar might be the case with 40 per cent of the respondents who said their status was equal to that of their parents-in-law. But for 40 per cent of those who ranked their status lower than that of their parents-in-law, two reasons may be advanced: One, the class status of the parents-in-law might be higher than that of the daughters-in-law. Two, even if the class or modern status of the daughters-in-law was higher than that of their parents-in-law, the respondents might have had respect and reverence towards the traditional status of the parents-in-law as older and respected members of the family. As far as the brothers-in-law and other members of the family were concerned, the working women had a higher edge in their perception. This is because, the traditional and modern (class) status of brothers-in-law and other members are likely to be low.

On the whole, it appears that there is positive change in the perception of self-status of working women in relation to other members of the family. However, the working women did not consider their status higher than that of their husbands. This is because most husbands had a status, both traditional or ascribed and modern or achieved, higher than their wives.

2. *Working Women and Freedom*

Individual freedom is the hallmark of democracy. The degree of freedom accorded to women reveals the degree of equality ensured to women in society. It was attempted to analyse the status of working women in terms of degree of freedom accorded to them. In this regard two factors were taken into consideration: 1) freedom to keep monthly salary to oneself and 2) freedom to buy / spend.

To a question as to where they (respondents) kept their salary every month, a maximum of 40 per cent said they handed over their salary to the husband, while 20 per cent said they gave it to their parents / parents-in-law. It showed that 60 per cent of the respondents had no individual freedom to own their hard-earned salary on which they had an absolute right. It was also found during discussion that most working women of this portion of the sample had to ask money for personal expenses. However, there were a few who were allowed to keep with them a certain portion of their salary. The fact that 60 per cent of the respondents were not allowed to keep their salary with them shows that a majority of the working women were deprived of their financial right.

Interestingly, 40 per cent kept their salary in banks, but were expected to spare 50 per cent of their salary for family expenses. This section of the sample enjoyed a certain degree of liberty and freedom. It may be concluded that a majority of the working women, under investigation, had no individual freedom as far as their right to own their salary was concerned.

3. Freedom to Spend/Use Salary

Another attempt was made to measure the degree of individual freedom with reference to six factors viz. ,

(a) Clothes, jewels, costumes etc. , for personal consumption,
(b) Domestic appliances
(c) Savings for children
(d) Personal LIC, FD etc
(e) Presents, gifts for relatives, friends and
(f) Parents' health, own brothers' / sisters' education or marriage

The respondents were asked to indicate the degree of freedom they enjoyed to spend or use their salary on the factors mentioned above.

1. Clothes, Jewels, Costumes for Personal Consumption

It was found from the data that as high as 50 per cent of the respondents were relatively very much free to spend a portion of their salary on clothes, jewels, etc for personal consumption. Similarly a majority of the respondents enjoyed a greater degree of freedom with regard to purchase of domestic appliances (50%), make savings for children (65%). It means that the respondents had a relatively greater degree of individual freedom to spend a portion of their salary on items connected with personal and family needs. However, the respondents had little freedom to invest in personal LIC, FD (40%) and spend on presents / gifts for relatives and friends, and much worse, the respondents (35%) had hardly any freedom to bear the medical expenses of their parents' or brothers' / sisters' education or marriage (20%).

From the above analysis the following conclusions may be drawn.

(1). The working women had a greater degree of individual freedom with regard to personal expenses, purchase of domestic items or investments for their children's future.

(2). But the working women had little freedom to make investments in personal LIC etc, or give presents to relatives or friends, or mear expenses' on parents health or brothers' / sisters' education or marriage. In short, the working women had freedom to spend a portion of their salary on their husbands' family, but they had no freedom to spend on their personal friends or relatives, including parents, and brothers and sisters.

4. Involvement of Working Women in Decision-making

The status of a woman largely depends on the extent to which she is involved in the decision-making process in the family and society. Numerous studies have concluded that there is an increased participation of working women in the decision-making process. (Indiradevi, 1974; Mohini Sethi; 1989; Prakash Rao and Nandini Rao, 1982. But a more rigorous research is needed in this regard. The present thesis has taken into account 1) The attitude of the respondents towards working women's ability to take independent decisions, 2) The attitudes of the husband and parents-in-law towards working women's ability to take relatively independent decisions and 3) The degree of involvement of working women in the decision-making process.

Working Women's Perception about Their Ability to Take Independent Decisions

As far as the attitudes of the working women about their ability to take responsible decisions are concerned, 80 per cent gave a positive reply. It means a majority of them believed that working women were capable of taking responsible decisions

Perception of Family members about Working Women's ability to take Independent Decisions

It may not be possible to come to any definite conclusions, on the basis of working women's perceptions alone. More important is how the working women's status-set members, such as husbands, parents-in-law, react to the issue. Thus a question was asked if there was considerable change in the attitudes of family members viz. husbands, parents-in-law, regarding the ability of the working women to take responsible decisions. According to the respondents, 80 per cent of the husbands had a favourable opinion about their ability to take responsible decisions. But the respondents were not sure about their parents-in-law as only 55 per cent of them (Parents in-law) were favourable, while 45 per cent were not. It means, the respondents felt that a greater proportion of husbands than parents-in-law had a more favourable opinion about the ability of working women to take responsible decisions.

Degree of Consultation

A final attempt was made to analyse the extent to which the working women were consulted by family members while taking important decisions. The respondents were asked as to how often they were consulted by their family members, such as husband and parents-in-law, while taking family decisions. As per our data, 60 per cent of the husbands consulted their wives very often in taking decision on vital issues. It means the husbands were relatively more democratic and liberal towards their wives. It indicated a substantial change in the status and role of working women. However, the parents-in-law were not much consulted very often and their attitudes ascertained. Interestingly, 30 per cent of the parents-in-law never consulted their daughters-in-law. It suggests a lack of harmony between the parents-in-law and the daughter-in-law in the family. It further showed that parents-in-law did not acknowledge the working status of their daughters-in-law. Our finding partly supports the Resource Theory of Power by Blood and Wolfe (1960). However, the fact that parents-in-law do not yet recognize the importance of working daughters-in-law shows the power of tradition. Our finding does not fully corroborate the findings of Prakash Rao and Nandini Rao (1982: 213) who came to conclusion that the employed mothers exercised more decision making power.

WORKING WOMEN AND SHARING OF DOMESTIC RESPONSIBILITIES

Traditionally, gender has been used as the basis of division of labour in the family and society. The main responsibilities of women were, and are, rearing children, doing domestic chores and looking after the young, aged, and relatives and guests. There was a clear-cut and neat demarcation of male and female duties.

Researchers have contended that gainful employment introduces significant changes in woman's traditional role and status (Blood and Wolfe, 1960). It was intended to examine whether or not employment brought about any significant changes in the domestic role of working women. In this regard two factors were considered:

1. Degree of help received from family members, and,
2. Contribution of help by family members with specific reference to areas of domestic chores.

1. Degree of Help extended by Family Members

The respondents were asked how often family members like the husband, mothers-in-law / sisters-in-law, servants helped in domestic chores.

It is important to observe that 60 per cent of the respondents felt that the husbands rarely helped, while 40 per cent said 'often' or 'sometimes'. It means, the husbands were not much cooperative with their wives in doing domestic works. The finding is corroborated by the finding of Hanumantha Rao (1990), who concluded that the traditional sex-specific division of labour did not seem to have changed very much in the families of working women. Prakash Rao and Nandini Rao (1982) also drew similar conclusions. But mothers-in-law and sisters-in-law extended a helping hand to working wives. Interestingly, working women received more help from servants than from other members of the family. It could be stated that employed women do not receive much help from their husbands in domestic chores, while close women relatives did help. But servants seemed to be the main helping hands for working women.

2. Working Women and Family Members' Help in Domestic Chores

Another attempt was made to assess family members' help in different areas of domestic chores. Domestic chores were divided into six areas viz.

1. Cooking and serving
2. Cleaning and washing
3. Domestic purchasing
4. Looking after guests and relatives
5. Accounts and payments, and
6. Care of children.

The data showed that 60 per cent of the working women either did the job of cooking and serving for themselves or took the help of close relatives. Twenty (20%) per cent of them received any help from the servants. Hardly 20 per cent of them received help from the husbands. Sixty (60%) per cent of the respondents were helped by the servants in cleaning and washing clothes and utensils, while 50 per cent received help in domestic purchasing from the husbands, 40 per cent did it for themselves. A majority of the working women looked after guests and relatives (60%) and maintained accounts and payments bills. Husbands' help was minimum. As far as care of children was concerned, only 40 per cent received help from the husbands. The remaining either themselves took care of the children or were helped by servants. The data clearly show that the traditional role of women viz rearing children, doing domestic works and looking after guests continues to be the lot of working women. It could be said that employment, far from helping working women, has added to the stress and strain as far as domestic chores are concerned.

5. Working Woman and Problems of Adjustment in the Family

Employment of woman brings in its train not only more income and economic security to the incumbent and the family, but also problems of adjustment with the family members. Employment of woman necessitates a redefinition and reinterpretation of roles and statuses of husband and wife on the one hand, and mother-in-law and daughter-in-law on the other. Employment introduces a clash of egos in the family. In this regard the following points were studied.

1. Superiority Complex of Working Women
2. Husband-Wife Relationship, and
3. Mother-in-law daughter-in-law Relationship.

1. Superiority Complex of Working Women

As high as 54 per cent of the respondents agreed fully with the question whether or not a working woman tended to look down upon non-working members of the family. Another 26 per cent also agreed partly with the statement. Hardly 20 per cent disagreed with the statement. It means clearly that almost 80 per cent believed that employment produced a superiority complex among working women. Of course, in one sense, it is good that working women should become conscious of their economic and occupational status. But at the same time employment generates class differentials between the employed and non-employed. Such a complex among working women may lead to interpersonal differences and clashes.

2. Husband - Wife Relation

It has already been stated that husband–wife relationship in Indian society is one of superiority and inferiority. But employment introduces new dimensions of equality between husband and wife. The employed woman is more likely to have differences of opinion on various issues. With this assumption, a question was asked whether or not there could be differences of opinion between husband and wife on family issues.

The data indicated that a majority of the respondents felt that there could be heated exchanges between husband and wife on matters like insufficient contribution of salary towards home expenses (75%), not paying enough attention to the needs of the husband (60%), neglecting overall family interests (55%) and not taking enough interest in the children (58%). It could be concluded that the working woman, due to employment, is not able to perform her wife-mother roles satisfactorily in the family.

3. Mother-in-law — Daughter-in-law Relationship

The relationship between mother-in-law and daughter-in-law has a significant bearing on the changing role and status of the working woman. Our aim was to find out the impact of employment on the mother-in-law – daughter-in-law relationship. The respondents were asked the following question: "It is believed that the working woman cannot adjust with her mother-in-law. Do you agree? If yes, give reasons". Reponses were recorded with regard to:

(1) Non-acceptance of mother-in- laws' superiority.

(2) Assertion of economic superiority

(3) Tendency to dominate others, and

(4) Tendency to separate from the parents-in-law

The analysis has revealed that a majority of the working women agreed that employed women tended to reject or question the traditional power and authority (85%) of the mother-in-law. Similarly, 72 per cent felt that working women tended to assert their economic superiority, while 55 per cent thought that employed women developed a tendency to dominate others, including the mother-in-law and finally 82% believed that employed women would tend to establish a separate household apart from the parents-in-law. It clearly shows that the employment of women is likely to produce dissensions between the mother-in-law and daughter-in-law.

The analysis of the role and status of the working woman has led to the following conclusions.

1. The working woman perceives a positive change in her status in relation to other members of the family but not the husband. Such a conclusion needs to be supported by further research by controlling class and age status of other members in the family.
2. Relatively speaking, the working woman is given individual freedom in matters of purchase etc. Nevertheless, she is not allowed to provide financial help to her siblings and parents. The working woman becomes the property of her husband in the family.
3. The working woman is relatively involved in the decision-making process. But the final decision still rested with the husband and elders in the family.

4. The working woman does not receive much help from the husband in doing domestic chores.
5. Employment of woman has given rise to problems of adjustment with members like the husband, mother-in-law/father-in-law and the in-laws.

We may state that it is early to conclude one way or another about the emerging status of the working woman in the family.

ROLE AND STATUS OF WORKING WOMAN IN OFFICE

The emerging status of the working woman is directly related to her role in the office. Our assumption is that since the working woman is new to office culture, she is likely to encounter problems of adjustment. She is likely to experience stress and strain in the office. The following indicators have been used to study the role and status of the working woman in office.

1. Working women's interpersonal relations with office staff
2. Working women and attitudes of office staff
3. Working women and union activities.

Working women's Interpersonal relations with office staff towards female workers as perceived by the latter. Attitudes, and subordinates towards working women, and working women and union activities.

Working Women and Interpersonal Relations with Men and Women Colleagues

Interpersonal relations between working women and men and women colleagues is significantly related to their performance of the office role effectively. The respondents were asked the following question: "In your opinion, with whom do working women frequently go for lunch and coffee, and chitchat during leisure the in office?" It is interesting to observe that 60 per cent of the respondents felt that working women had more frequent contact with women than with men. But 60 per cent had frequent contact with men colleagues, too. This indicated that the working women in our sample were relatively conservative as they were constrained by gender biases and prejudices.

Working Women's Efficiency in Relation to Men and Women

Another attempt was made to measure the attitudes of the working women in relation to men and women in office. Such an analysis would help us in knowing whether the respondents felt that they could work more efficiently with men or with women. Data collected in this regard revealed that 50 per cent of the respondents felt that they would be working more efficiently with women than with men. But 60 per cent felt that they could work with men less efficiently. It means, women workers gave first preference to women and second preference to men as colleagues. This again lends support to our assumption that working women are not very much favourably disposed to working with men. Such an attitude on the part of working women acts as a hindrance in their integrating themselves with office culture.

1. Attitude of Working Men towards Working Women's Abilities

Working women's status in office depends upon how they perceive themselves in terms of punctuality, efficiency, social behaviour and hard work in relation to men. Data showed that a majority of the respondents felt that their degree of performance in office was lower than that of men. For example, 50 per cent believed that their degree of punctuality in relation to men was low. But 30 per cent contended that their punctuality was equal to that of men.

This indicated that 30 per cent felt that working women were as punctual to office as men. Similarly, 42 per cent felt that their efficiency in office was lower than that of men, while 35 per cent ranked their as efficiency equal to that of men. Forty per cent (40%) of the respondents believed that their social behaviour in terms of free mixing with men and women was lower than that of men, while 40 per cent felt that they were as sociable as men. As far as capability hard work in office was concerned, 50 per cent believed theirs was lower than that of men, while 25 per cent felt it was equal to that of men. From the above analysis the following conclusions may be reached:

1 On the whole, the working women felt that their performance, measured in terms of punctuality, efficiency, social behaviour and hard work, was lower than that of men.

2. Nevertheless, there is a substantial change in the perception of the working women with regard to their performance in office.

2. *Working Women and Attitudes of Office Staff*

The status enjoyed by working women at the work- place is relative to the attitudes held by the office staff. To be more specific, it is a question of whether or not the working women receive respect, sympathy and co-operation in discharging their office duties from their staff.

1. Attitudes of Superiors

The respondents were asked to indicate the attitude of their superiors towards themselves in office in terms of respect and sympathy, co-operation and mutual help and differences of opinion.

(a) Respect and Sympathy

As high as 60 per cent of the respondents said that they

received respect and sympathy to some extent, while 25 per cent said it was to a great extent. It means the higher authorities did not have much respect and sympathy for subordinate women. Many respondents felt that they were being discriminated against at the hands of their superiors.

(b) Cooperation and Mutual Help

The majority (55%) of the respondents said that they received little co-operation and mutual help from their superiors, while 23 per cent admitted they were never given co-operation and mutual help from their superior officer. It means, the higher authorities did not have a favourable attitude towards the working women.

(c) Differences of Opinion

When asked whether the respondents had any differences of opinion in office matters, 50 per cent said that there were differences of opinion between them and the boss.

The above analysis clearly showed that the attitudes of the superior officers were not favourable towards the working women.

Attitudes of Men Colleagues Towards Working Women

We have so far analysed the attitudes of superior officers towards working women. A similar attempt was made to get to know the attitudes of men colleagues towards working women.

The relationship between colleagues is one of equality. The performance of employees depends upon the question how far colleagues interact with each other with mutual trust and confidence. In the case of working women, their sex factor (being women) may influence the relations between men and women employees. The respondents were asked to indicate the attitudes of men colleagues towards themselves with reference to three factors viz. , 1) Co-operative and helpful 2) Indifferent and non-cooperative, and 3) Uncooperative. An overall assessment of the data revealed that relatively, men colleagues exhibited an indifferent attitude towards working women. For example, 65 per cent received co-operation and help from their colleagues to some extent". With regard to other factors. 40 per cent said that their colleagues were indifferent and non-cooperative on many occasions. Another 35 per cent also said that generally men colleagues were indifferent and non-cooperative. But 50 per cent of the respondents expressed the view that their colleagues were positively uncooperative to a great extent or very often. On the whole, men colleagues, according to working women, were not very favourable towards them. This indicated that working women had yet to make efforts to adjust with office culture.

3. *Attitude of Subordinates*

Like the attitudes of superiors and colleagues, the attitudes of subordinates such as peons and other lower staff plays an important role in determining the performance of working women in office. An analysis of subordinates' attitudes towards working women showed a favourable approach. For example, 50 per cent said that the subordinates were co-operative and helpful to a great extent, while 28 per cent said they were so only to some extent. It means, for 78 per cent of the respondents, the subordinates were co-operative and helpful. Similarly, a majority (50%) said that the subordinate were never indifferent and un-cooperate. But 50 per cent and 20 per cent respectively did say that they were not indifferent and non-cooperate generally, or they were so only occasionally. In other words, for 50 per cent of the respondents, the subordinates were indifferent and un-cooperative and for the other 50 per cent, they (subordinates) were not. With regard to un-cooperative attitude of the subordinates, a majority (70%) said "never". That means the subordinates were never un-cooperative. On the whole, the subordinates were relatively cooperative and helpful, not indifferent and un-cooperative.

Working Women and Office Related Functions

Employees are social beings. Their social status in office not only depends upon how they discharge their duties in office, but also how they involve themselves and take active part in office related programmes, meetings, functions such as marriages, anniversaries, birthdays, picnics etc. Participation in such functions will strengthen interpersonal relations among the staff members and thereby boosts one's image in peer group circles. An attempt was made to analyse how often and how best working women took part in social functions. The respondents were asked to indicate their involvement in programmes like 1) Get-togethers, picnics, 2) Birth days, marriage anniversaries, poojas.

1. Get-togethers, Picnics

Working women's participation in social functions like get-togethers and picnics arranged by the office staff was minimal. As high as 55 per cent of the respondents rarely participated in social functions; of the remaining 45 per cent, 25 per cent were regular, while 20 per cent attended occasionally.

2. Farewells, Annual Gatherings

The participation of women employees in farewells, annual gatherings was equally low as only 28 per cent attended such functions very often, while 24 per cent often enough. It means, 52 per cent generally took part in farewells and annual gatherings. But 48 per cent rarely attended such functions. According to the respondents, it was not possible for them to spare time, due to family difficulties.

3. Birth Days, Marriage Anniversaries, Poojas

Unlike the above two types of programmes, a majority of

the respondents attended social functions like birthdays, marriage anniversaries, as a maximum of 48 per cent attended the above named functions very often, while 22 per cent said often enough. It means, 70 per cent of the respondents were interested in birthdays, marriage anniversaries, poojas which involved religious and spiritual ceremonies. The reasons advanced were that participation in such functions brought Punya or merit. It may be concluded that by and large, working women evinced less interest in social functions arranged by their office colleagues. However, they evinced more interest in social functions with a religious and spiritual significance.

Working Women and Union Activities

Workers' unions / associations are integral parts of social, economic, occupational, legal and political organizations, unions as pressure groups play a significant role in promoting the interests of its members by their bargaining strength vis-à-vis the Govt. or management. In this connection the following factors were studied:

1. Membership of Union,
2. Reasons for becoming or not becoming a member of the union, and
3. Participation in protest programmes.

Membership of the Union

According to the data, the respondents were not keen on becoming members of the staff union. A maximum of 53 per cent were members of the union, as against 47 per cent who did not become members.

Reasons for Becoming or not Becoming Members

When asked to furnish reasons for becoming members of the union, the respondents gave the following reasons

1) Friends pressured them (40 %); 2) the unions helped

in redressing injustice (38%); and 3) they promoted unity and organization (27%). It could be gauged from the data about the strength union membership that 70 per cent had a clear vision of the importance of unions.

Of those who were not members of the union, 50% did not believe in the union as a means of securing justice, while others were not interested in such activities. Our casual discussion revealed that parents, husbands, kith and kin did not want working women to become union members.

Participation in Union Activities

Participation of working women in union activities was analysed by taking into consideration the following factors:

1. Protests, submission of memos
2. Strikes, bandhs, processions
3. Hunger strikes

1. Protests, Submission of Memos

The data have shown that only 26 per cent were ready to participate in protests and submission of memos very often, while 30 per cent said often enough. It means, on the whole 56 per cent of the respondents were interested to register their protest against injustice. But a maximum of 44 per cent were not ready to take part in protests and submission of memos.

2. Strikes, Bandhs

A majority of the respondents (68%) were not prepared to take part in strikes and bundhs. They said it was risky and dangerous for working women to involve themselves in strikes and bundhs. But 32 per cent expressed their desire to take part in union activities involving risks and dangers. This change needs to be recorded.

3. *Hunger Strikes*

Hunger strike is the last resort of any programme of agitation to exert pressure on the Govt. / management. In this regard, hardly 25 per cent were willing to take part in hunger strikes as against 75 per cent who were not at all ready to be involved in such hazardous activities.

To sum up; in the last chapter we have tried to analyse the status of working women in office. In this regard the following conclusions may be drawn.

1. Working women maintained friendly and harmonious relations more with women than with men in office.
2. The respondents felt that men workers had a poor image of working women as being less punctual, efficient, sociable and hardworking in comparison with men.
3. Higher officers (men) had negative attitudes towards working women. Men colleagues did not have an attitude of co-operation and mutual help. But the subordinates had respect and sympathy for them.
4. Working women could not take active part in social functions arranged by the staff. But they attended marriages and poojas.
5. Most working women did not take active interest in union activities. It could be concluded that the working woman is not yet integrated with office culture.

Main Findings

1. The working women, by and large, came from Hindus, towns and cities, upper and middle classes. A Majority of them were married and had children. A greater proportion of them were living in joint families. A greater proportion were highly educated and engaged in higher occupations.

2. Husbands of the respondents were highly educated and were engaged in bureaucratic and professional jobs.
3. The parents of the respondents held graduate and postgraduate degrees and were serving in white-collar jobs. The parents-in-law of the respondents came from a poor educational and occupational background.
4. The working women in the sample showed a favourable and positive attitude towards higher education and employment for women. According to them, education will help women become a better wife and mother. It could be said that there is a change in the perception of working women regarding their status. Modernisation in terms of education and employment is well within the tradition. However, working women are found to be relatively traditional with regard to marriage and family. Although there is a change in the attitudes towards seeking divorce from the husband under unbearable conditions of torture and ill-treatment, generally they upheld the ideology of marriage as a sacrament. Similarly, a majority wanted the youth to have freedom in choosing their life-partner to some extent, yet they held that parents and other kin-members' approval and sanction are essential. This indicated a desire for arranged marriage. They were also found to believe in the dowry system. There was a positive attitude towards remarriage of young widows, preferably having no children. But middle-aged widows with children re-marring was viewed with disapproval. Widow remarriage is still regarded as a sin. A majority of them have accepted the small family norm through family planning. But the desire for a male child is very strong. Couples with only daughters were

reluctant to undergo tubectomy or seemed depressed if they had gone the operation.

A joint family comprising ego's parents, wife, small children and unmarried sisters and brothers is a common phenomenon. Married brothers tend to live separately. In short, the working women were relatively traditional in their attitudes towards marriage and family. The status and role of working women is closely tied with the ideology of marriage and family.

5. The working woman perceived a positive change in her status in relation to other members of the family but not the husband. But such a conclusion needs to be supported by further research by controlling intervening variables such as class, age, rural / urban background of the other members in the family.
6. The working woman is relatively given individual freedom in matters of purchase etc. Nevertheless, she is not allowed to provide financial help to her kith and kin. The working woman, thus, becomes the property of her husband in the family.
7. The working woman is relatively involved in the decision-making process. But the final decision rested with the husband and other elders of the family.
8. The working woman does not receive much help from her husband in doing domestic chores. In joint families, she is being helped by women members, while in nuclear families by servants. The traditional division of labour between men and women in the family does not seem to have changed significantly.
9. Employment of woman has given rise to problems of adjustment with members like the husband, and mother-in-law. Therefore, it is not possible to come

to any conclusion about the emerging status of the working woman in the family.

10. The working woman was found relatively conservative in her attitude towards men workers in the office. She maintained friendly social contacts more with women than with men. Such a conservative attitude might affect her discharging of duties in the office.
11. The respondents felt that men workers had a poor image of the working woman as less punctual, efficient, social and hardworking in comparison with men.
12. The working woman did not enjoy higher status in the eyes of men staff superiors and colleagues. However, the subordinates (men) had sympathy for her.
13. The working woman could not take active part in social functions arranged by the staff. But she did attend marriages and poojas. This also indicated her relative alienation from office staff.
14. The working woman did not take active interest in union activities. It could, thus, be concluded that the working woman is not yet integrated into office culture.
15. Finally, we can draw the conclusion that the working woman's status is in transition, as her social background and role and status-sets are relatively conservative. Although education has made her more conscious of her individuality. and employment has given her economic security, she is not yet recognized by the members of the family on the one hand, and office staff on the other.

Bibliography

Agarwal Mamta, *Education and Modernisation*. Endersearch, New Delhi, 1986.

Agnew Vijay, *Elite Women in Indian in Politics*, Vikas Publishing House, New Delhi. 1979

Agnew Vijay, 'A Review of the Literature of Women'. *Journal of Indian History*, Vol. 55, No. 1-2, 1977

Ahmad Karuna 'Studies of Educated Working Women in India: Trends & Issues, *Economic & Political Weekly*, Vol. XIV, No. 33, (August) 1979.

Ahmad Karuna,'The Trishankus Women in the Profession in India' *Sociological Bulletin*, Vol. 33, No. 142, (Mar, Sept.) 1984.

Ahuja S.R. 'Practice and Problem of Dowry', *Social Defence*, No. 17, 1982.

Altekar A.S. *'Position of Women in Hindu Civilisation'*, Motilal Banarasidas, 3rd edition, Varanasi, 1962.

Anderson & Shills 'Modernisation and Higher Education in Modernisation', in *The Dynamic Growth*, Myron Weiner (Ed.), Voice of America, U.S.A. 1966.

Andharga Janaki *'Husband's Role Expectation of their Wives'* Masters Thesis, Tata Institute of Social Science, Mumbai. 1983.

Andre Beteille, 'The Position of Women in Indian Society' In Devaki Jain (Ed.), *Indian Women*, Govt. of India New Delhi, 1975.

Anna Mathew, *Dowry and its Various Dimensions*, 1990.

Bharat Debi, *Middle Working Women of Culcutta*, Probartak Printing & Halfton Ltd., Culcutta. 1988.

Bhatty I Bhatty J. 'Demographic Portraits of Professional Women in *Indian Educated Women in Indian Society*'. Tata McGraw Hill, Mumbai, 1977.

Bhoite Anuradha, *Women Employees and Rural Development*, Gian Publishing House, New Delhi, 1987.

Bhushan L.I., *Concern for Status Among Educated Women*, Classical Publishing Company, New Delhi, 1983.

Biswanath Mukerjee, 'A Multi Dimensional Conceptalisation of Status of Women', *Social Change*, Vol. 5, Nos. 1&2, Mar – June, 1975.

Blood & Wolfe *Husband and Wives*, The Free Press of Glencoe, New York, 1960.

Blood R.O., *Love Match and Arrange Marriage*, The Free Press, New York, 1967.

Blood Ro Jr 'Husband–Wife Relationship'. in the Employed Mother in America (Ed) by Nhy F Ivon & Halfmon, LWr & McNolly & Company, Chicago, 1963.

Blood Robert and Hamblin, Robert L., *The Effect of the Wife's Employment on the Family Structure*, The Free Press, New York, 1968.

Blumber RL&Leela Dwark, *'India's Educated Women'. Options and Constraints*, Hindustan Publishing Corporation, New Delhi ,1980.

Boserup Ester, *Women's Role in Economic Development*, George Allen & Unwin Ltd., London, 1970.

Chetana Kalbagh, *'Women, Employment and the Work Place'*, Discovery Publishing House, New Delhi, 1992.

Chen, M.A , 'Introduction' in M.A. Chen (Ed.), *Widows in*

India. Social Neglect and Public Action, Sage, New Delhi, 1998.

Chitra Ramchandran, *'Maternal Employment and Education Development of Children'*, Commonwealth Publication, New Delhi, 1989.

Choudhary, J.N., *'Divorce in Indian Society'*, Print Well, Jaipur, 1988.

Cook A., *'The Working Mothers'* Cornels University, New York, 1975.

Corwin L.A., 'Caste and Class and the Love Marriage; Social Change in India'. *Journal of Marriage & Family,* Vol. 39, 4, Nov. 1977.

Desai N. & Anontrom S., 'Middle Class Women's Entry into the World of Work'. Indian Standard Institute, Culcutta, 1985.

Desai N. and M. Krishnaraj, *'Women and Society in India,* 'Ajanta Publisher, New Delhi, 1987.

Desai Neera, *'Women in Modern in India,* 'Vora and Co. Publishers Pvt. Ltd, Mumbai, 1977.

Desai Neera, *Indian Women, Change and Challenge in the International Decade,* Popular Prakashan, Mumbai, 1985.

Devis K., *Human Society,* The Macmillan Company America (USA), 1970.

Dhingra, O.P., *'Women in Employment'*, An unpublished report of Sriram Centre For Industrial Relations & Human Resources, Chapter II, New Delhi, 1972.

Dowell E.M., *'Family Development'*, Chicago J. B. Lippincott Co.,1963.

Dube S.C., 'Modernisation and Its Adaptive Demands on Indian Society' *Paper in Sociology of Education in India,* (Ed) Gere etc. NCERT, New Delhi, 1967.

Dube S.C., 'Men's & Women's Roles in India, *'Women in the New Asia* (Ed) Barbara E Ward, Paris: UNESCO, 1963.

Dube S.C., *'Indian Village,* Routlege & Kegan Poul', London, 1955.

Dube S.C. *Contemporary India and Its Modernisation,* Vikas Publication, New Delhi, 1974.

Edmund W. Overstreet, *'The Biological Make up of Women',* McGraw Hil, New York, 1963.

Eleanor E. Maccoby, *Women's Intellect in the Ptential of Women,* Ives Washbon Ina, New York, 1961.

Emerson R.M., 'Power Dependence Relations', American *Sociological Review,* Vol. 27, Feb

Emile Durkheim, 1956.

Fonesca M.B., 'Marital Separation Disorganisation of seen through an Agency'. *Sociological Bulletin,* March, 1964.

Fonesca M.B., 'Family Disorganisation and Divorce in Indian Communities', *Sociological Bulletin,* 1963.

Fonseca Mabel, *Counseling for Marital Happiness,* Manaktalas, Mumbai, 1966.

Ghosh S.K., *Women in a Changing Society,* Ashish Publishing House, New Delhi, 1984.

Giriraj Gupta, 'Love and Arranged Marriage and the Indian Social Structure'. *Journal of Comparative Family Studies,* Vol. VIII, 1 1976.

Giriraj Khanna, *Indian Women Today,* Vikas Publication, New Delhi, 1978.

Glueck & Glueck E., 'Working Mothers and Delinquency,' *Mental Hygiene,* 12 (July 1957).

Goode W.Hil J., *World Revolution and Family Patterns,* The Free Press, New York, 1957.

Gore M.S. 'Education and Modernisation', In *Essays on Modernisation of Under Developed Societies,* Vol. II, (Ed.), A.K. Desai The Atur & Company Mumbai, 1971.

Gore M.S., *Urbanisation and Family Change,* Popular Prakashan, Mumbai, 1968.

Gupta G. *'Family and Social Change in Modern India', Main Currents in Indian Sociology,* Vikas Publication, New Delhi.

Gupta S.S., *A Study of Women of Bengal,* Indian Publication, Culcutta, 1970.

Hanumantha Rao M., 'Employment of the Wife & Husband's Participation in House Work'. *Indian Journal of Social Work,* Vol. III, July 1990.

Hate, C.A., *'Changing Status of Women in Post - Independence India'*, Allied Publisher, Mumbai, 1969.

Heer, Devid M., 'Dominance and the Working Wife', *Social Force,* Vol. XXXV, (May 1958).

Hotler 'Sere Roles and Social Change '. In *Acta Sociology,* Special issue on See Roles 14: 1-2-1971.

ICSSR, *Status of Women in India,* Allied Publication, New Delhi, 1975.

Indiradevi M., *Women – Education Employment Family Living, A study of Emerging Hindu Wives in Urban India,* Gian Publishing House, New Delhi, 1987,

Indrajeet Kaur, *Status of Hindu Women in India,* Chugh Publication, Allahabad, 1983.

Inkeles, 'Making Men Modern on the Causes and Consequences of the Individual Change in Six Developing Countries', *AJS,* 75: 2: 208 225, New York, 1969.

J.S., Augustine, *The Indian Family in Transition,* Vikas Publication, New Delhi, 1982.

Jain Shashi *Status and Role Perception of Middle Class Women,* Pooja Publisher, New Delhi, 1988.

Jha, K.N., *'Women Towards Modernisation'*, Janaki Prakashan, Patna, 1985.

Kala Rani, *'Role Conflict in Working Women*, Chetana Publications, New Delhi, 1976.

Kapadia, K.M., 'The Family In Transition'. *Sociological Bulletin*, 8 September 1959.

Kapadia, K.M., *Marriage and Family in India*, 2nd Edition, Oxford University Press, Mumbai, 1958.

Kapur Promilla, *Marriage and Working Women in India*, Vikas Publishing House, New Delhi, 1970.

Kapur Promilla, *The Changing Status of the Working Women In India*, Vikas Publishing House, New Delhi, 1974.

Kapur Promilla, *Love Marriage and Sex*, Vikas Publication, New Delhi, 1973.

Kapur Rama, "Role Conflict Among Employed House Wives," *Indian Journal of Industrial Relations*, Vol. 5, No. 1, July 1969.

Khanna G. & Varghese M.A., *Indian Women Today*, Vikas Publication, New Delhi, 1978.

Klein V. Bretains, *'Married Women Workers'* Routledge & Kegan Paul, London, 1965.

Kliger D., *'The Effect of the Employment of Married Women On Husband and Wife Roles*, 1954.

Kraisonswasdi Napasri, *Women Executives A Sociological Study in Role Effectiveness*, Rawat Publication, New Delhi, 1989.

Krishnaraj M., *Women and Science: Selected Essays*, Himalaya Publisher, Mumbai, 1991.

Kumud Ranjan, *Women and Modern Occupation in India*, Chugh Publication, Allahabad, 1993.

Kurian G., *A Review of Marriage and Adjustment in Indian Families*, Vikas Publications, New Delhi, 1982.

Lalita Devi, U., *Status and Employment of Women in India,* B.R. Publishing Corporation, Delhi, 1982.

Landecker W.S., 'Class Crystallization and Class Consciousness, *American Sociological Review,* Vol. XXVIII, (1963).

Lenski G.E., 'Status of Crystallization: A Non Vertical Dimensional Social Status,' *American Sociological Review,* Vol. XIX (Aug. 1954).

Linton Ralph, *'The Study of a Man; An Introduction,* Appleton Century Crofts , New York, 1964.

Lowie, R.H., *'Primitive Society'*, Rotledge and Kagan, London, 1913.

Macelland, D.C., *'The Achieving Society,* D. Van Nostrand Co. INC Princeton, 1961.

Mahajan Amarjeet, 'Women's Two Roles: A Study of Role Conflict, *Indian Journal of Social Work,* Vol. 26, No. 4, January 1966.

Mahajan V.S., *'Women's Contribution to India's Economic & Social Development'*, Deep & Deep, New Delhi, 1989.

Majumdar & Madan 1980

Malika Veena 'The Study of the Middle Class Working Women in Kanpur, *The Indian Journal of Social Work,* Vol. 21, Dec. 1960.

Malinowski B., *Crime and Constonin Savage Society,* Routledge & Kagan Paul, London, 1949.

Mamdoni, *The Myth of Control,* New York Monthly Review Press, 1972.

Manjula R. *'Unmarried Working Women: Marriage Career,* Radiant Publisher, New Delhi, 1990.

Maslow A.H., *Motivation and Personality,* Harper and Row, 1954.

Mathur Deepa, *Women Family and Work,* Rawat Publication, New Delhi.

Mehta Rama, *'The Western Educated Hindu Woman,* Asia, Mumbai,1970.

Merton, *'Social Theory & Social Structure,* Amerind Publication, New Delhi, 1972.

Milton Singer, 1956.

Mishra Rajendra, 'Working Women – A Frame of Reference.' *Indian Journal of Social Research,* Vol. 18, No. 2 & 3, 1977.

Mishra Sangeeta, *'Status of Women in Changing Urban Hindu Family,* 1993.

Mukherjee, 'A Multidimensional Conceptionalisation of Status of Women '. Social Change Vol. 5, No. 1 & 2, March 1975.

Murichan J. 'Women in Kerala, Changing Socio - Economic Status and Self Image'. A Desouza, (Ed.), In *Women Contemporary India,* Manohar Publication, 1977.

Nagesh H.V., 'Widowhood In India', *JSS,* Dharwad, 1988.

Nair P.T., *Marriage & Dowry in India,* Minerva India, 1978.

Nandi, D. Ashis, *Indian Women From Pardah to Modernity,* Vikas Publication, New Delhi, 1976.

Nath K., 'Women in the Working Force in India'. *Economic & Political Weekly,* No. 11, 1968.

Nayar Usha, *Women Teachers in South Asia,* 1988.

Parson T., 'Age and Sex in the Social Structure of the United States'. *American Sociological Review,* October 1942.

Prakash Rao & Nandini Rao, *Marriage, the Family and Women in India,* Heritage, New Delhi, 1982.

Pratima Kumari, *Changing Value Among Young Women,* Amar Prakashan Publisher, New Delhi, 1988.

Prakash Rao & Nandini Rao, 'The Dowry System in Indian Marriage, Attitudes Expectations and Practices'.

International Journal of Sociology of the Family, No. 10, 1980.

Ragunandhan Reddy, *Changing Status of Educated Working Women,* B.R. Publishing Corporation, New Delhi, 1986.

Rajagopalan, C., 'Role Perception and Role Performance'. *Indian Journal of Social Work,* Vol. 34, No. 1, 1965.

Rajaraman I., 'Economics of Bride Price and Dowry' *EWP,* Vol. 18, No. 8, 1983.

Rajmohini Sethi, *'Modernisation of Working Women in Developing Societies'*, National Publishing House, Jaipur, 1976.

Ralph Linton, *'The Study of the Man: an Introduction'*. New York, 1964.

Ramanamma, A., *'Graduate Employed Women in an Urban Setting'*, Dastane & Dastane, Pune, 1979.

Ramu, G.N., *Women Work and Marriage in Urban India,* Sage, New Delhi, 1989.

Ranade, S.N. & *'Women and Employment'*. Ramchandran TISS, Mumbai, 1970.

Rao Venkatu & V. Sudershan, 'Continuity & Change in Marital Choice'. *Social Action,* Vol. 28, 15 March 1978.

Rao, V. Prakash & 'Arranged Marriage: An Assessment of the V. Nandini Rao Attitude of the College Student in India'. *Journal of Comparative Family Studies,* Vol. VII, 2 August, 1972.

Ross A.D., *The Hindu Family in its Urban Setting,* Oxford University Press, New Delhi, 1973.

Ross Aileen, D., *The Hindu Family in the Urban Setting,* The University of Toronto Press, Toronto, 1961.

Sachchidananda, *Tradition, Modernity and Modernisation in India,* Indian International Publication, Allahabad, 1976.

Sandhya Maliya, Women Professionals in Hyderabad, Department of Sociology, University Hyderabad, 1992.

Sengupta P., Women Worker in India, Asia Publishing House, Mumbai, 1960.

Sethi R.M., 'Status and Power of Rural Women'. In R.K. Sapra (Ed), *Women & Development*, Ashish, New Delhi, 1989.

Shabbarwal, S., 'Women in Organisations'. In R.K. Sapra (Ed), *Women Developments*, Ashish, New Delhi, 1989.

Sharma Anita, 'Modernisation and Status of Working Women in India '. Mittal Publication, New Delhi, 1990.

Shastri, S., 'Women in Vedic Age'. Bharatiya Vidya Bhavan, Mumbai, 1962.

Singh, K.P., "Career and Family – Women's Two Roles". *Indian Journal of Social Work*, Vol. 33, No. 3, October 1972.

Singh, K.V., 'Status of Women and Population Growth in India'. Munshiram Manoharlal, New Delhi, 1979.

Sinha Pushpa, *Role Conflict Among The Workng Women*, Anmol Publications, New Delhi, 1987.

Srivastava Vanita '*Employment of Educated Married Women in India*, National Publishing House, New Delhi, 1978.

Sur A.K., *Sex and Marriage in India: An Ethno historical Survey*, Allied Publishers, New Delhi, 1973.

Talwar Usha, *Social Profile of Working Women*, Jain Brothers, Jodhpur, 1984.

Thomos P., *Indian Women Through The Ages*, Asia Publication, Mumbai, 1964.

Tod James, *Annal & Antiquities of Rajasthan*, Vol. II, Oxford University Press, London, 1920.

Uplaonkar, A.T., *Rural Youth in Modern India*, Uppal Publishing House, New Delhi, 1998.

Uplaonkar, A.T., *Social Background and Occupation Aspirations of College Students*, Ajanta Publications, New Delhi, 1988.

Upreti, H.C. and N. Upreti, 'Parental Authority and Attitudes of Women Students Towards Marriage & Dowry', *Indian Journal of Social Work,* Vol. 43, 3. 1982.

Upreti Nandini, 'The Changing Status of Women in India,' In Sushil Agarwal (Ed), *Constitutional Provision & Social Reality,* Print Well, Jaipur, 1988.

Usha Devi, R., *Divorce to Women: Socio–Psychological Problems,* APH, New Delhi, 1988.

Wood M.R., 'Employment and Family Change: A Study of Middle Class Woman in Urban Gujarat, *Social Action,* Vol. 25, (3) 1975.

Appendix

INTERVIEW SCHEDULE

CHANGING ROLE AND STATUS OF WORKING WOMEN IN MODERN INDIA: A CASE STUDY OF EDUCATED WORKING WOMEN IN GULBARGA CITY

I. SOCIAL BACKGROUND OF THE RESPONDENCE

1. Name :
2. Age :
3. Religion : (1) Hindu
   (2) Muslim
   (3) christian
   (4) Budhist
   (5) Jainism
   (6) Other
4. Caste:
5. Education:
6. Completion of:

VILLAGE	TALUKA CITY
7TH	P. U. C.
8TH	B. A.

7. Place of Birth: (1) Rural (2) Urban
8. Marital Status: (1) Married (2) Unmarried

(3) Widow (4) Divorce

(5) Deserted

II. FAMILY BACKGROUND OF THE RESPONDENTS:

9. Type of family : (1) Joint (2) Nuclear
10. Father's : (1) Education ______________
    (2) Occupation ____________
11. Mother's : (1) Education
    (2) Occupation
    (3) Income
12. Father-in-laws : (1) Education
    (2) Occupation
    (3) Income
13. Mother-in-law : (1) Education
    (2) Occupation
    (3) Income
14. Husband's : (1) Education
    (2) Occupation
    (3) Income
15. If the respondent has Children :

Sl. No.	Name	Age	Education	Occupation
1.				
2.				
3.				
4.				
5.				
6.				

16. Traditional occupation of the family:

17. Total Income of the family ______________ p. m.

III. EDUCATIONAL BACKGROUND AND ATTITUDE OF WOMEN TOWARDS EDUCATION

18. In your opinion what are the aims of higher education with regard to women

    1) Make them play woman's traditional role of wife
    2) Make them fit for modern life
    3) Enable them to seek employment

19. In your opinion how much education should women be given?

    1) High School
    2) PUC
    3) Graduation
    4) Post Graduates

20. Do you think educated women will become better wives?

    (1) Yes (2) No

21. Do you think educated women will become better mothers?

    (1) Yes (2) No

22. Do you think educated women can better manage their homes?

    (1) Yes (2) No

23. Do you think educated women can accept changes easily?

    (1) Yes (2) No

24. Do you think educated women are more social?

    (1) Yes (2) No

III. WOMENS ATTITUDE TOWARDS EMPLOYMENT

25. Professional qualification:
26. Designation ________________ Department __________
27. Salary Rs. ____________p. m.
28. Since how long have you been working in this job?
    ___________ years ___________months.
29. Where you working before marriage?
    (1) Yes (2) No
30. If not then how man years after marriage did you start working?
    ____________years.
31. How much financial assistance are you contributing to your parents per month?
    Rs.__________ p. m.
32. How much financial assistances are you contributing to your husband's family per month?
    Rs. ___________ p. m.
33. Do you keep money for personal expenses every month?
    (1) Yes (2) No
34. In your family who motivated you to get into employment?
    (1) Parents (2) In-laws (3) Husband (4) Any others

V. REASONS FOR TAKING UP EMPLOYMENT:

35. What are the main reasons for taking up the job?
    1) Want to support myself
    2) Raise the standard of the family
    3) Secure economic independence

36. Do you think employment of girl help in finding a suitable partner?

    (1) Yes (2) No

VI. WOMEN'S ATTITUDE TOWARDS MARRIAGE AND FAMILY?

37. If married, age at marriage?

    ________ years.

38. In your opinion at what age a women should marry?

    ________ years

39. Who takes decision for setting marriage?
    1) Parent's choice without the consent of the self
    2) Parent's choice with the consent of the self.
    3) Self Choice with the consent of the parents.
    4) Self-choice without the consent of the parents.

40. If women are given full freedom to marry, what form of marriage they adopt?
    1) Love marriage
    2) Arranged marriage
    3) Arranged marriage with freedom of choice

41. If you had to make a choice between pursuing career and getting married, what would you choose?
    1) Career
    2) Marriage
    3) Both

42. Do you think education of girls helps in finding a suitable partner?

    (1) Yes (2) No

43. Do you think that marital happiness and satisfaction

are lesser among employed wives than among the unemployed?

(1) Yes (2) No

VI. DOWRY

44. Do you think dowry is necessary for marriage?

(1) Yes (2) No

45. If yes, give reasons

1) It is prestige issue
2) It is a custom
3) It gives respect in the in-laws family
4) Provide security for brides

46. Do you think that employed women are exempted from payment of dowry in marriage?

(1) Yes (2) No

47. Have your parents offered dowry at your marriage?

(1) Yes (2) No

48. If yes specify reasons?

1) In laws family demanded
2) It was good proposal
3) To assist in laws family
4) If any, specify

49. If dowry is not offered, what consequences do you expect?

1) In laws do not ill-treat
2) Husband does not care
3) Exploitation in-laws family

50. Do you prefer to give or accept dowry for the marriage of your son / daughter?

    (1) Yes (2) No

VII. WIDOW – REMARRIAGE:

51. Do you favour widow remarriage?

    (1) Yes (2) No

52. If yes, give reasons:
    1) Nothing is wrong in remarriage
    2) Opportunities must be given for a fresh beginning in life:
    3) Women must get equal rights
    4) If widow's are not re-married immorality spreads
    5) It is in to deprive women of their sexual rights
    6) If any, specify: ________

53. If not, specify reasons:
    1) It is against the customs
    2) Children born of widows remarried will have to face problems later in their life.
    3) If any, specify:

54. In your opinion should a widow re-marry if she has children?

    (1) Yes (2) No

55. If yes, give reasons:
    1) ________________
    2) ________________
    3) ________________

55. If not, why?

1)

2)

3)

56. In your opinion should a working widow remarry?

(1) Yes (2) No

57. If yes, give reasons:

1)

2)

3)

58. If not, why?

1)

2)

3)

VIII. FAMILY PLANNING

59. Are you aware of family planning programme?

(1) Yes (2) No

60. If yes, how did you come to know?

1) Propaganda
2) Family planning workers
3) Friends, relatives etc.

61. Do you believe in family planning?

(1) Yes (2) No

62. If yes, why?

1) It helps to have small family
2) It secures a higher economic standard
3) Health of parents and children is protected
4) It reduces population pressure

63. If not, why?
    1) It is against God's will
    2) Good will provide food, clothing and shelter to every one.
    3) Reduce capacity of hard work
    4) Children are God's Gift
64. How many children should a woman have?
    1) One
    2) Two
    3) Three and more
65. What should be the minimum age difference between children?
    1) 2 years
    2) 3 years
    3) 4 years
66. Do you think that the birth of male child is essential for a family?

    (1) Yes (2) No
67. Have you adopted family planning measures?
68. If yes, mention measures
    1) Spacing
    2) Condomy
    3) Sterlisation
    4) Copper T.
    5) Tubectomy / Vasectomy
    6) Any other specify
69. If not, why?

70. Do you prefer to live either in the joint or nuclear family?
    1) Joint Family
    2) Nuclear Family
71. If joint family, why?
    1) Living together is strength
    2) Provide economic security
    3) Property could be kept intact
    4) Helps intimes of social and economic crisis.
72. If Nuclear family, why?
    1) Greater freedom to live one's own life
    2) Provide a higher standard of living
    3) Provides better education, food, clothing and housing to its members.
    4) Cannot adjust with other family members
73. Do you want to help members living in joint/nuclear families? If yes, how?
    1) Help financially in times of family needs like education, marriage
    2) Help in times of illness etc
    3) Participation in life-cycle
74. Do you thing employed women should live with their in-laws?

    (1) Yes (2) No

1) If yes, reason 2) If not, reasons

75. If the working women are living with their in-laws, do you think the in-laws will be happy about their daughter in-laws employment?

    (1) Yes (2) No

IX. STATUS AND ROLE OF WORKING IN FAMILY

76. As a working women, how do you perceive your position in the family in relation to other members?

Relationship Perception of Position

High Equal Low

1. Husband
2. Parents-in-law
3. Brothers-in-law (Employed)
4. Others

77. Where do you keep / deposit your salary every month?

1) With the Husband
2) With Parents / Parents-in-law
3) With Oneself

78. How free are working women to spend / pay from their salary on the following items?

1) Clothes, jewels costumes for personal consumption
2) Domestic appliances
3) Savings for children
4) Personal LIC, F. D. etc
5) Present, gifts for relatives, friends
6) Parents' health own brothers / sisters' education or marriage

79. Do you think working women can take responsible decision in their life?

1) To great extent
2) To some extent
3) Never

80. Do you think there is a considerable change in the attitude of your family members viz, husband, parents-in-law towards the ability of working women to take responsible decisions?

To great extent To some extent Nil

Husband

Parents-in-law

81. How often are you consulted by your family members such as husband and parents-in-law, while family decisions are being taken?

Very Often Often Enough Never

Husband

Parents-in-law

82. How often the following members extend a helping hand in your domestic chores?

Very Often Often Enough Rarely

Husband

Parents-in-law

Servants

83. In your day-to-day domestic chores what is the contribution of your family members?

Husband Mothers/Sister-in-law/self

Servant

Cooking and Serving food

Clearing and washing

Domestic purchasing

Looking after guests & relatives

Accounts and payments

Care of Children

84. It is often believed that a working woman tends to

look down upon non- working members of the family, Do you agree?

1) Agree fully
2) Agree partly
3) Don't agree

85. Do you think that there could be differences of opinion between the working woman and her husband on family issues? If yes, specify the issues.

Yes No

1. Not sufficient contribution of salary for home expenses
2. Not paying enough attention to the needs of the husband
3. Neglecting overall family interest
4. Not taking enough interest in children

86. It is believed that the working woman cannot adjust with her mother-in-law, Do you agree? if yes, give reasons.

Yes No

1. Non acceptance of mother-in-laws superiority
2. Economic Superiority
3. Tendency to dominate others
4. Tendency to separates from parents-in-law

X. STATUS OF ROLE OF THE WORKING WOMAN IN OFFICE

87. In your opinion, with whom do working women frequently go for lunch and coffee, and chitchat during leisure in office?

Very Frequently Frequently Never

Men

Women

88. In your opinion, with whom can working women work efficiently-men or women?

More Efficiently Less Efficiently Not Efficiently

Men

Women

89. How do you rates the performance of working women according to the factors given below in comparison with men workers?

Higher Equal Lower

Punctuality

Efficiency

Social Behaviour

Hard Work

90. In your opinion, what is the attitude of higher authorities towards working women in office?

To Great Extent To Some Extent Never

Respect and Sympathy

Co-operation and mutual help

Differences of opinion

91. In your opinion, what is the attitude of (men) colleagues towards working women in office?

To Great Extent To Some Extent Never

Co-operative and helpful

Indifferent & non-co-operative

Un co-operative

92. In your opinion, how do lower men staffs react towards working women?

To Great Extent To Some Extent Never

Respect and Sympathy

Co-operation and mutual help

Differences of opinion

93. In your opinion, how often do working women take active part in office related functions?

Very Often Often Rarely

Get together picnics

Farewells, annual gatherings

Birthdays, marriage anniversary poojas

94. Are you a member of the staff union?

1) Yes

2) NO

95. If yes, what are your reasons?

1) Pressure of Friends

2) Helps in redressing injustice

3) Unity and organization

96. What are your reasons for not becoming members?

1) I am junior

2) Unions do not serve any purpose

3) Not interested

97. In your opinion, how often do working women take active part in union activities to protest against injustice by the management / Govt.?

Very Often Often Rarely

Protests, submission of memos

Strikes, bundhs

Hunger strikes

Index

N

O

P

R

S